"RATTLE AND SHAKE"

THE STORY OF THE BERMUDA RAILWAY

"RATTLE AND SHAKE"

THE STORY OF THE BERMUDA RAILWAY

BY

David F. Raine

POMPANO PUBLICATIONS

BERMUDA * CANADA * ENGLAND

FIRST EDITION 1992

International Standard Book Number: ISBN 0-921962-08-8

Other Books by David F. Raine
PITSEOLAK — A CANADIAN TRAGEDY
ARCHITECTURE BERMUDA STYLE
SIR GEORGE SOMERS — A MAN AND HIS TIMES
BERMUDA, AS IT USED TO BE
THE ISLANDS OF BERMUDA — ANOTHER TIME
THE PREGNANT FATHER
GUIDE TO HISTORIC ST. GEORGE

Cover design by the author

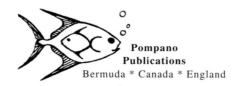

**Pompano
Publications**
Bermuda * Canada * England

TABLE OF CONTENTS

In a country which abounds with natural beauty, very few of man's inventions have pulled at the emotional chords of the Bermudian people in the way that old "Rattle and Shake" did. This was the affectionate name given to the Bermuda Railway, the first true form of modern mass public transport to be introduced into these islands since official settlement first commenced way back in 1612.

Although it has long since passed into the annals of local history, mention of the railway continues to evoke a certain sense of passion. The merest reference to it releases a flood of reminiscences from those parents and grandparents who remember riding the trains; and it inspires dreams among those who still try to imagine what it must have been like to be drawn through the countryside and along the shoreline in the 1930's.

Today, the Bermuda Railway is not much more than a fading memory. The tracks which once stretched from Somerset to Hamilton and then on to St.George have long since gone. Even the fragmented 'Railway Trail', which seeks to lure residents and visitors back along its picturesque path, is only ever but a piecemeal journey into nostalgia. The sections of the railway's once bustling route are disjointed and some are sadly overgrown, partially obliterated by alternative land developments and the various distractions and debris of the Modern Age. Some parts, like that which led out of Hamilton and along the North Shore towards Flatts Village, have been redesigned entirely, so that younger generations will always have known it as "Palmetto Road". Only rarely do souvenir hunters manage to find one of the many thousands of hand wrought spikes or metal plates, which kept the rails securely fastened into place.

This book does not claim to be the definitive history of 'The Bermuda Railway Company'. That will come later through the labours of other researchers. Rather, it seeks to tell the story of a railway, one which for only a few short years shuffled its way from one end of Bermuda to the other. Hopefully, the present volume also reflects some of the social impact which it had on these islands; an impact which helped to change the country's physical and emotional make-up forever.

As usual, I need to acknowledge the help provided by Grace Rawlins and the staff in the Reference Rooms of the Bermuda Library, in Hamilton. Similarly, I wish to thank John Adams and the staff at the Government Archives; they have not only located relevent primary sources but also secured permission to reprint photographic material and maps. Without their collective knowledge and generous assistance, all research would be considerably more arduous.

Finally, each of us owes a special debt of gratitude to Rosa Hollis. The fascination which she and a small group of enthusiasts have shown for the railway, over many years, has helped to preserve its memory. Her unique musuem near Flatts, appropriately housed in a former station, remains the sole visual testimony to its existence.

David F.Raine
Bermuda - 1992

LIST OF ILLUSTRATIONS

LIST OF ILLUSTRATIONS

NOTE

Many of these photographs are from various collections deposited with the Bermuda Archives. They are reproduced with the permission of the Archives and individual credits are given on appropriate pages. Research and identification of these items has benefited from the patience and kind assistance of Sandra Rouja, Research and Collections Assistant.

The two maps are based upon a single map located in the Archives. After a thorough search of that facility and the Bermuda Reference Library in Hamilton, the original publisher and its date of printing remain unknown. It is believed to have been included in promotional material distributed to tourists in the late 1930's. This map has been redesigned by the author and is presented here as two separate sections.

Postcards of the Bermuda Railway and copies of Bermuda Railway tickets are from the collection of Jill Amos Raine and are reproduced here with her permission.

All other photographs were taken by the author in 1992.

An Unfortunate Beginning

During the opening years of the twentieth century, the mutual mind of the Bermudian public and its legislators, tended to regard all ideas of mass transportation with guarded caution.

Accustomed to tranquil lives which centred upon horses, carts, boats and carriages, not everyone was convinced that there was any real need to replace such traditional and proven modes of transport, particularly with mechanical forms which had still not established themselves as being either reliable, or viable. Indeed, the very thought of having a railway system for such a small cluster of unconnected islands appeared to be so fanciful and frivolous that it was invariably dismissed as being completely absurd.

Among farmers, merchants and politicians alike, conversation on the subject of trains was instinctively merged with the broader discussion about the acceptance of that other, equally as dubious innovation - the motor car. Not everyone could accept that those ridiculously noisy and awkward-looking vehicles might prove eventually to be one of the most significant inventions of the twentieth century. On the contrary, there were many who doubted that such wretched, uncomfortable contraptions could possibly outlive any usefulness beyond that of carrying platoons of doomed soldiers into the front lines of battle. That the motor car might become a popular form of travel for individual families seemed totally nonsensical.

On these remote sub-tropical islands, trains were viewed with similar caution and scepticism. Always held somewhat disdainfully at arm's length, they were perceived to be neither necessary, nor desireable. Loyal supporters adamantly presented the counter-argument that railways were being operated quite successfully in other countries and in places just as small as Bermuda. However, even the most ardent proponents privately admitted that they too harboured a deep-rooted reluctance to sacrifice the song of the cardinal, or the clicks of the cicadas, for the inevitable rumbles, clangs and screeches which were known to accompany every engine which had ever been built. Opponents protested that among these blue Bermuda skies there was no place for billowing clouds of black smoke; nor was there any desire to replace the gentle swaying of oleander hedges with the shuddering vibrations of railway compartments being tugged across the landscape on meandering iron tracks.

The first suggestion that Bermuda might benefit from building its own railway had been made in 1893. This proposal was formulated and presented to the Governor by an American resident named Mark Golinsky, then living in St. George.

On 30th. June 1893, Mark Golinsky forwarded a petition to Governor Thomas C. Lyons, asking that the Council and Assembly of Bermuda consider granting him authorization "to do business in these Islands for the purpose of owning, building and equipping a complete line of electrical transportation through Bermuda", through a business to be named 'The Bermuda Electric Railway and Lighting Company'. He gave sworn assurance that the complete financial funding for the venture would come from private investments already secured from his own considerable resources and "several of my wealthy friends residing in America and

England." It would not cost the people of Bermuda one single penny and the Government would not be required to make any monetary commitments whatsoever.

Golinsky's proposal was visionary indeed. In addition to guaranteeing a network of trains extending from Somerset, to Hamilton and on to St. George, it also included a plan to install electric lighting along the entire length of the route, with the potential to extend electricity into every area and every home at a later date. The latter was indeed an attractive bonus.

Without doubt, the petition was a carefully prepared document, one which went significantly beyond the mere proposal of an idea. With impressive attention to detail throughout, it even selectively itemized the route to be taken by the tracks. In surveying this intended route, Mark Golinsky and his associates deliberately tried to keep to existing roadways as much as possible; this was, in part, an attempt to diplomatically avoid any major disruptions to land or life. It was, of course, also significantly more cost effective. From the town of St. George the tracks would pass along the south side of St. George Island and proceed all the way up to, and across the Causeway. From Blue Hole Hill it would follow the North Shore Road all the way into Flatts where, in order to prevent any major demolition or construction within the village itself, a bridge would be built across the northern rim of the inlet. Skirting Flatts, Golinsky's plan allowed for the train to proceed along the existing North Shore Road up to Mount Langton, on the outer edge of Hamilton. It would then carefully pass down onto Front Street. From a custom-designed depot in central Hamilton, the railway would then exit the capital along the Middle Road in Paget and then head directly through the western parishes of Warwick and Southampton and out to Mangrove Bay, in Somerset.

It was a meticulously prepared submission; one which appeared to anticipate most eventualities. Along the Causeway, for example, the scheme called for electric wires to be stretched beneath the bridge in a manner designed not to interfere with the passage of boats. Also, although single tracked, the company indicated its intention to build sidings and passing bays at intervals throughout the length of the railway track; stations would be erected wherever and whenever they might be deemed appropriate and necessary. Finally, as a splendid gesture of goodwill and public relations, Mark Golinsky's company also offered to reimburse the Bermuda Government for the salary of the bridge keeper and to provide any practical and technical assistance "as may be required to prevent any inconveniences or danger to the public."

In exchange for so generously offering to provide the country with both a railway system and an electrical grid, at no financial costs to the Bermudian Government, Golinsky requested that all building materials, power plant equipment and other related machinery be allowed to enter the country duty free for the period of twenty-five years. Similarly, he wanted to be extempted from all Colony, Parish and Corporation taxes for a like period of time. Additionally, the petition required free license to erect pillars, posts and other apparatus such as the Company should see fit and necessary in order to ensure the efficient operation of the railway.

Golinsky and his nameless coterie of business backers undertook to lay the first mile of track within three years of the passing of the required Act of Incorporation and "to complete the same as rapidly as possible." Upon completion, they committed themselves to providing a minimum of three passenger trains and two freight trains each day, with "as many more as the business may require." There was even a provision permitting the transfer of the entire railway network over to the joint governments of Britain and Bermuda, in the event of hostilities, to be used for the exclusive benefit of "the transportation of passengers, troops, guns and whatever purpose desired". The only condition was that it should be kept in sound operational order until such times as it might be returned to the Company.

For all of its generosity and wisdom, "The Bermuda Electric Railway and Lighting Company" nevertheless expected several additional, major concessions from Bermuda and her people; ones which went well beyond conventional tax relief. It was reasonable that it should seek the protection of exclusivity for its efforts; that was an obvious and readily agreeable concession. However, there were several thorny areas in the overall proposition which the Government of the day was reluctant, or unable, to freely barter. It could, of course, neither abandon its responsibilities nor sell its soul, even when lured by such exciting innovative prospects as the introduction of a railway and electricity. How, for example, could the Executive Council be expected to issue a private company with a carte blanc permit to purchase all pieces of land "as may be needed" for those sections of track which did not travel along existing roadways? Furthermore, how could the Governor possibly approve the succession of two hundred feet of land and water north of Flatts, "for building and battery storage purposes and other purposes as they may see fit connected with their said business"? Asking the House of Assembly to give away bits of Bermuda in that way, to foreign investors no less, would be clearly tantamount to treachery.

Nevertheless, Mark Golinsky's petition was quite persuasive and included one passage devoted entirely to highlighting the benefits which all of Bermuda could reap from having a railway system. He noted that he had become personally enamoured with the natural beauty of these islands and, as a resident, had come to intimately understand their requirements and capabilities. Addressing the good sense of Governor Thomas C. Lyons and members of the Council and Assembly, he noted that he had become acutely aware of the urgent need to inject fresh capital into the economy. Large investments, he submitted, were essential to the country's prosperity and would "make them one of the finest spots on the face of the globe, situated as they are in the midst of the Atlantic, in such a position that they are free of the extremes of the cold of the North and the fervid heat of the Torrid Zone." He contended that Bermuda could very well develop into being one of the most popular tourist resorts in this part of world and suggested that an effective system of rapid transportation, radiating from the centre of the islands, would enhance its appeal to visitors — enabling them to travel to "all areas on excursions with speed and comfort, and return to their hotels at night with safety."

Presenting a logical sequence of well-balanced arguments, he mentioned the obvious benefits which would be afforded to the island's scattered garrisons and the ease and efficiency with which troops might be moved from one posting to another. Also emphasized were the clear advantages which trains could have to farmers seeking to convey produce to market as speedily as possible; he foresaw trains stopping so close to fields of onions that sacks could be loaded directly aboard and then whisked away onto the docks within minutes of their having been plucked from the soil. The railway would also prove beneficial to the Government, he maintained, by providing a unique service capable of improving the speed and effectiveness of communications between various administrative departments and their field officers.

On the surface, it was apparently all too good to be true. But, then, nobody doubted that Mr. Mark Golinsky was indeed a truthful and honest man, one whose radical ideas certainly deserved further consideration. Therefore, after eloquently laying his proposals before Governor Lyons, he left printed copies of his petition in the hands of those who could give it the due attention which he humbly maintained that it warranted. After which, he retired to the tranquility of his home in St. George and patiently awaited the outcome of their deliberations.

Progress was far less rapid than he hoped. Approaching their summer recess, the island's parliamentarians were still locked in debates over the Quarantine and Public Health Acts. In the wings of the political stage, Mr. George Spurling was eagerly awaiting his cue to introduce 'The Board of Immigration Report'; after this, 'The Goals Establishment Bill', the 'Savings Bank Act' and the controversial 'Fish Net Bill' were already scheduled for discussion. In the Legislative Council, the Honourables W. H. Gosling, J. H. Trimingham, T. N. Dill and W. H. Wilkinson were trying to resolve the claims dispute between the steamship 'Orinoco' and the S. S. 'Alpha'. Furthermore, they had just appropriated three thousand pounds for road repairs and were hardly in the mood to turn their minds to ripping it all up again for some train track.

The petition was also slow in moving among the appropriate Government offices. A brand new map of Bermuda had just been published by 'Farnworth', of New York, and many of the clerical staff were already busy trying to arrange for distribution of this, as well as the latest set of Admiralty Charts, to the country's shops. Other officers were trying to gather information on the reported occurrence of a disease among lemon trees; they needed to nip that in the bud.

Golinsky's petition was finally brought forward for mention on 14th. July 1893. It was presented to the Legislative Council by the Honourable T. N. Dill and Chairman R. D. Darrell tentatively scheduled preliminary discussion for the following Tuesday, 18th. July. Then, it was deferred in order to enable passage of the 'Treatment of Criminal Lunatics Bill'. Finally, when all obstacles seemed to have been cleared, Governor Lyons opted to take his annual vacation, commencing on 27th. July. Since he was not expected to return until 4th. September, interim Administrator Samuel Pym, carefully delayed all debates until that time. The railway proposal had been placed on the back burner; now the stove temporarily was turned off altogether.

In the seclusion of his home in St. George, Mark Golinsky watched summer turn into autumn; and by year's end his proposals had still received little more than passing attention. With the dawning of a new year, the House discussed the needs for dredging the Southampton Channel and became bogged down with finding practical solutions for an alternative entrance into St. George Harbour. There were heated debates about salaries for prison officers, followed by spirited disputes over the best methods of inspecting imported fruit and vegetable produce. Repaving the streets of Hamilton proved to be equally as contentious and time-consuming. The House next granted priority to contemplating Dr. Smith's suggestion that a silkworm industry might be developed and, subsequently, several sessions were devoted to anticipating potential problems associated with the local cultivation of mulberry trees. There was also time to lament the passing of Major-General Sir Frederick Chapman, a former Governor of Bermuda.

Apparently, the moment never seemed to be quite right for the country's leaders to properly address the Golinsky Petition. So it was that with the end of winter season in 1894, he quietly boarded a ship and returned to New York. With him went the enthusiasm for a scheme which had proposed revolutionizing not only the entire transportation network of these islands, but would have rewoven its economic fabric as well. Nearly three decades would pass before those pioneering ideas resurfaced, but Mark Golinsky had long since gone.

By a stroke of historical irony, at precisely the same time that Bermuda was procrastinating over the introduction of a railway, in 1893, the Parliament in distant British Guiana was busy discussing viable ways that could open the forested hinterland and enable the development of its latent mineral resources. Indeed, one wise Guyanese legislator already had quietly suggested that a railway link between the mines and the coast would probably be the most effective means of achieving that objective. He would have his wish, fifty years later — with the purchase of discarded trains and track from the Government of Bermuda.

The Growing Need for Change

For the next three decades, very little was ever said about a railway; the name of Mark Golinsky faded away altogether and was soon forgotten. In the interim, Bermuda mourned the death of Queen Victoria; there was the exciting distraction of having several hundred scruffy, rebellious, bearded Boer War prisoners living out on some islands in the Great Sound. Mark Twain visited, left and died. The country opened its first Bioligical Station at Agars Island, and proudly applauded its sons as they went off to be bombed and gassed in the quagmires of Ypres, Flanders and the Somme.

However, probably far more significantly than the collective importance of these and other individual events, the entire mood of the country was subtly undergoing some drastic changes. Changes which were far more profound than mere cosmetic surgery. There were now several distinct differences between Bermuda in the 1920's and those earlier days of 1893, when Mark Golinsky had tried fruitlessly to convince the country's leadership that railways should be adopted. Of paramount importance was the fact that the economy was on the brink of being completely restructured: the traditional agricultural and seafaring base was about to be replaced by one orientated towards tourism.

The dominant power behind this move was the worldwide shipping line of 'Furness Withy', which proposed developing the island's potential as a tourist destination on a scale never previously envisaged. The directors of this firm saw their principal role as that of carrier; ensuring that hundreds of American and Canadian visitors were brought regularly to Bermuda each week. However, they also saw it as their fringe responsibility to make certain that adequate 'quality' accommodation was available for their clients, once they arrived. To this end, 'Furness Withy' offered to become involved with the implementation of a comprehensive programme of hotel and other related developments. In conjunction with the Government, Bermuda's first major cruise ship policies were formulated and a comprehensive plan evolved whereby these islands would be transformed into a tourist resort.

With its avowed commitment to bringing cruise ships into the East End, 'Furness Withy' became directly and indirectly involved with such projects as the upgrading of the 'St. George Hotel', the construction of 'Castle Harbour' and 'Mid Ocean'. As part of an overall programme to expand and service the interests of the tourists, land was also acquired for the landscaping of two full-size golf courses adjoining these latter two hotels. For its part, the Corporation of St. George was inspired to organize and implement a full daily ferry schedule across the harbour and into the town, so that the visitors could enjoy sightseeing trips to Bermuda's oldest settlement; the old 'White Horse Inn' was refurbished, as was the 'Globe Hotel'. A couple of tea houses were opened.

As soon as the Bermuda Parliament accepted the general principal of constructing a railway, in 1922, a full feasibility study was undertaken by a recognized expert in this field, Mr. W. T. Foxlee, of London. Working in conjunction with Director of Works Mr. P. N. H. Jones, the fieldwork was completed by the end of that summer and the 'Report on a Light Railway' was presented for discussion on 28th. October 1922. The document presented the carefully reasoned opinion that, from a practical point of view, the railway project was entirely viable. Foxlee's Report, therefore, smoothed the final obstacles which had been blocking the advent of Bermuda's own 'Railway Era'. The country was on the brink of making perhaps the most dramatic change in its history, and certainly the most significant since the capital was moved from St. George to Hamilton.

The 1920's became a decade of unprecedented optimism as the country braced itself for the anticipated influx of visitors. On 11th. August 1924, even Arthur Haycock of 'Whitby' at Bailey's Bay, announced that the famous "Wonderland Cave", conveniently located in his back garden, would again be open to the public after a nine year closure. He advertised the luring excitement of "taking people 65 feet beneath the surface of the earth!" and then waited patiently for customers to come off the Causeway from St. George. With a new road planned from Tucker's Town, he could even anticipate customers arriving from the luxury hotels being build out there. Of course, with a train he would do substantially more business.

Throughout the early stages of this period of economic rejuvenation, the need to introduce a more effective means of transportation was addressed in earnest. 'Furness Withy' repeatedly emphasized the necessity of being able to carry visitors speedily to other destinations within Bermuda — Hamilton, "Devils Hole', Horseshoe Bay, Somerset and so on. Convenient, rapid transport, it was argued, was the key to having them see the beauty of the islands and enjoy a complete vacation.

However, although the exciting prospects promised by increasing tourism undoubtedly provided an impetus to change, Bermudians themselves had already come to recognize that travelling within their own country had reached levels of intolerable, disjointed inefficiency.

There was general agreement that the entire issue demanded serious confrontation, as opposed to the easier approach of procrastination. In particular, the public had come to accept that Hamilton and St. George were both becoming far too congested. The carts and carriages of import/export agents were having an increasingly dangerous effect on pedestrians who, in turn, were already having to negotiate a steadily growing number of cyclists furiously pedalling along the roads. On days when ships were fastened along Front Street, passengers and shoppers had to jostle their way through the chaos of hooves and wheels. Horses on the Hamilton dockside, frightened at being hemmed in by piles of crates and the squeezing proximity of other carriages, often reared at each other and occasionally kicked bystanders. Cyclists grazed shoppers trying to cross near Penno's Wharf in St. George; others slipped on rising mounds of manure and slithered indiscriminately into the path of friends and foes. In the country, deeply rutted tribe roads caused delays for farmers struggling to meet shipping deadlines; private carriages often got stuck or tipped over altogether.

It was painfully obvious to everyone that something inevitably would have to be done to facilitate the movement of traffic and eliminate the undesirable side effects which the bustling and congestion were starting to have on the daily lives, and temperaments, of those who lived here. The compelling necessity of resolving this chaos was abundantly clear to all.

Therefore, by the 1920's, it had become blatantly apparent that some type of so-called modern transportation would have to be introduced. The only real debate was over which form might best serve the interests of the community as a whole.

In offices, fields and coffee houses, the topic dominated conversation among salesmen, labourers, mothers and executives alike. Everyone, of course, saw solutions from a very individual perspective. Merchants from Fairylands and Paget considered that the automobile was the most sensible vehicle to satisfy their own personal requirements; farmers from Southhampton supported lorries as the best method for transferring bulk produce to market; St. David's Islanders were content to replace the oars of their rowing boats with motorized engines, and retain the traditional ferries. Dissident traders with shops and warehouses adjacent to the wharfs completely countered these views and could see absolutely no need to disrupt the existing arrangements whatsoever. Indeed some could foresee that any form of mass transport — whether it be cars, trolleybuses or trains — would be a distinct obstacle to the prevailing ease of simply hand-carrying boxes of goods across the road. A minority, lamenting the imminent demise of bygone days, commented that deliveries were always done by bike; ladies had carriages and fishermen had boats. Why change anything?

Unlike the tenuous days when Mark Golinsky had struggled to pioneer a railway in Bermuda, the 1920's represented an era when its introduction was far more timely. Not only was it plain that trains could furnish Bermuda with some obvious economic advantages, but train-travel as a broad concept had steadily secured international acceptance as an effective means of public transport. Golinsky's 1893 petition had been somewhat handicapped by an absence of supporting statistics; now, an abundance of evidence was available to prove their reliability and safety. Even the minimal mileage of track required within Bermuda was no longer seen as a restrictive obstacle. Cities like London, New York and Paris had developed railway systems to serve their own limited urban requirements and, although these were essentially subterranean networks, each had proved that railways could be successfully operated as financially viable entities, even when confined to smaller distances. The fallacious public perception that trains only ran between major towns, or had to link opposite sides of entire continents, was fast becoming redundant.

Whilst the automobile continued to enjoy growing and favourable support as the vehicle of the future, the trolleybus was seen initially to be the probable form of public transport most likely to enter Bermuda. However, on 4th. January 1922, the "Royal Gazette and Colonist Daily" featured a very lengthy article opposing the introduction of such buses. Reporting the outcome of a study which had been conducted by that paper's staff, it noted that partially based upon "the kindness of a visitor, we are in possession of many pictures and articles relating to the cost and operation of this modern means of transport." Referring to the condition of roads where they had been tried in America and elsewhere, the writer remarked that those in Bermuda "would not stand up to the wear and tear of the trolleybus", the buses were heavier than anything currently employed in Bermuda and it was considered impossible that local roads could withstand the ravages and destruction experienced elsewhere.

The newspaper also offered a similarly dissuading opinion about operating automobiles on these islands: "we find too that the cars used in America, since the roads are specially prepared for the existing motor traffic, are very much larger and heavier than is necessary or advisable here." In the streets, Bermudians reeled with horror at the thought of having to widen roadways and and then cover them with some special form of tarred surfacing.

Proponents of the railway gathered to substantiate their position. Some noted that since the introduction of trains in Switzerland, that small European country had experienced a sensational expansion of tourism. Others maintained that if "Furness Withy" was willing to make commitments to Bermuda's tourist trade, then the least the Government could do would be to respond by endorsing the installation of a railway. The local newspaper seemed to promote this attitude by publishing a host of details garnered from the annual report issued by the 'Virginia Railway and Power Company'. For its meagre 14 miles, that company had operated 22 'Birney Safety Cars' during the year ending 30th. June 1921. Delighted auditors revealed that only .0213 cents was now budgeted for track maintenance per mile; an additional .0162 cents was required for the upkeep of carriages, per mile. After exploring such operating costs as wages, power, damages, legal expenses and other overheads, the company was reporting small but satisfactory profits.

Other railway enthusiasts provided figures detailing costs of one small North American route whose tracks covered only 3.36 miles of existing streets. For initial total construction costs of $130,000, the operators had secured regular clientele numbering thousands of passengers every year. With each person being charged fares of just 7 cents and 5 cents, according to class of travel, that particular company estimated that it was now earning $173,281 per year — whilst having to pay out maximum operating costs of just $76,533 for the same period. Shareholders were delighted.

In its wisdom, Parliament passed 'The Motor Car Act 1921', with amendments designed to temporarily limit motorized vehicles to use of motorbuses. In consequence of that legislation, a committee had been appointed to monitor developments in related matters. In a brave demonstration of impartiality, the Honourable S. S. Spurling requested exemption from serving on this and similar committees; he was unashamedly among the most ardent supporters of the motor car. Salisbury Stanley Spurling was heir to a small family fortune based mainly on the hauling business established in St. George by George Spurling. He knew only too well how poor George had laboured heavily in the 1880's, using a small fleet of donkey carts to carry rubble and packages within the town; half an century later, the Hon. S. S. Spurling understood how much more could have been achieved had he enjoyed the benefits of a just few lorries!

National sentiment, however, tended to swing more favourably towards the idea of having a railway and there was a call that such a scheme should be thoroughly investigated by a team of experts, rather than relying upon the prejudices of untechnical locals who had perhaps no experience whatsoever with trains and their operation.

There was even tacit support for the railway from visitors, who had reacted harshly to the possibility that Bermuda's charm might become desecrated by the automobile. At a popular guest house named 'Westbury', in Hamilton, the visitors' book displayed a variety of unsolicited comments made by Americans who had stayed there: "Your island will be completely spoilt!" "What a crying shame to have motors here!" "This is certainly no place for cars — your roads are too narrow and winding!" "It is one of the chief attractions of Bermuda that we can drive in comfort and safety, without cars!" In a 'Letter to the Editor' printed in January 1922, hotelier Mary R. Tucker wrote: "With the motor terror once again looming on our local horizon, we should also take notice of the tourists' attitude towards such vehicles, for they have had experience with the things!"

The carriage evil is still with us!" cried an editorial in 1922. "The majority of the drivers have only one object in view — the docks — and what happens to unfortunate pedestrians or cyclists en route is a matter of indifference to them!" As a remedial measure, the newspaper called for the widening of the entrance to East Broadway — a prophetic plea which would go unanswered until 1992!

In Italy, Fascists clashed with Communists in the city Bologna; Britain condemned the sale of Gainsborough's "Blue Boy" to American Henry E. Huntingdon; the price of sugar fell in Havana to $7.25 per hundredweight; Japan and Washington were locking horns over the use of submarines; and the Prince of Wales was in Rangoon, receiving "an unbroken roar of cheering" from Burmese crowds. Meanwhile, Bermuda anguished over questions of public transport.

In 1922, a parliamentary debate approved the development of a railway, in principal only; however, no financing was forthcoming and no assured sources could be immediately identified. However, within a hectic two years, funds were indeed secured and, on Monday 4th. August 1924, a definite move was made towards realizing this dream, when the Legislative Council convened to formally address the first "Bermuda Railway Company Act."

For such a momentous decision, the day was noticeably inauspicious. The House of Assembly had met for only twenty-five minutes, during which the 'Public Officers Leave and Relief Act 1923' was discussed, alongside the awarding of a pension to Stanley Martin — a Government employee who had lost a foot in an accident. Mention of the pioneering 'Railway Act' was sandwiched between the "Wireless and Telegraphy Act" and an 'Acquisitions Resolve'. When it was mentioned again four days later, on the 8th. August, it was reluctantly at the expense of time allocated to the "Tucker Town Road Act" and debate on steamship, contracts being negotiated with 'Furness Withy'.

Nevertheless, Bermuda had opted finally in favour of operating its own railway and when Acting Governor Lieutenant Colonel C. W. Biggs R. E. rose to porogue Parliament on 20th. August 1924, his speech pointedly included reference to a hope that the country might now proceed forward "to the wishes for the realisation of the aims of the 'Bermuda Railway Company Limited'."

It may have been divine intervention that passage of this legislation should have proved to be rather low key, because there were several news items which surfaced at this particular moment which would have added superstitious fuel to die-hard opponents of the railway. To these darker minds, such events were bad omens forewarning that already trains were doomed. For example, at the precise moment that the Act was being passed in Bermuda, on 4th. August 1924, the New York Bus System was announcing its intention to expand into Manhattan. A spokesman said that buses were a serious rival to trains and would eventually drive them either above or below the streets thereby freeing the streets for individual cars. On 10th. August in New Brunswick, Canada, Frank Cornell, Chairman of the Board of Railway Commissioners, suddenly dropped dead at his farm outside St. John. Simultaneously, a glum Sir Henry Thornton, President of the Canadian National Railways, was predicting losses for the year of up to $15 million — based largely on reductions of business into the Great Lakes area and diminishing trade with America.

It was against this rather demoralizing backdrop that 'The Bermuda Railway Company' commenced surveying routes and prepared to lay the first lengths of track.

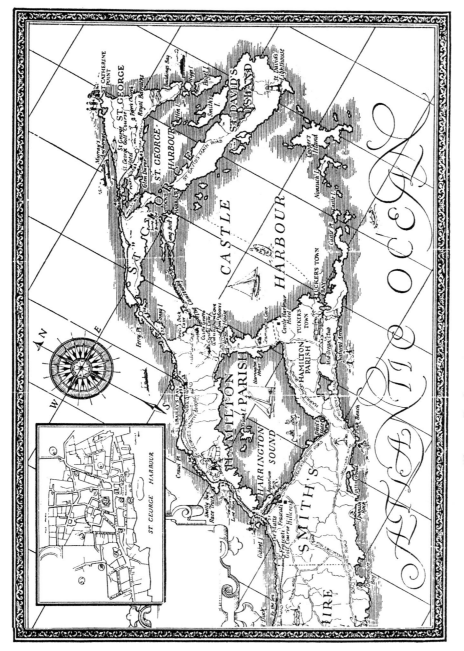

Key to Railroad Stations Numbered on Map

23. Serpentine Rd	31. Holly Hill	37. Coney Island
26. Race Course	32. Aquarium	38. Ferry Point
27. Pond Hill	33. Shelly Bay	39. West India Oil Docks
28. Prospect	34. Crawl Hill	40. Muller Bay
29. Devonshire Rd	35. Baileys Bay	41. Wellington
30. Store Hill Rd	36. Baileys Bay	42. St. Georges Terminus

1. The Eastern Route of the Bermuda Railway

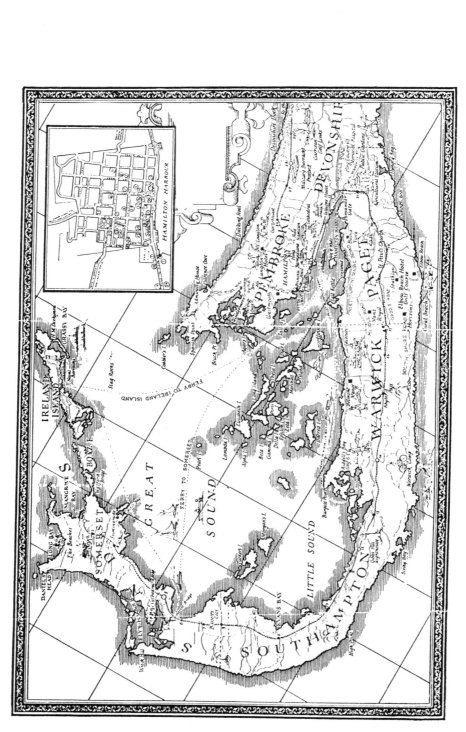

Key to Railroad Stations Numbered on Map

1. Somerset Terminus
2. Broom Street
3. Scotts Hill Road
4. Sound View Road
5. Somerset Bridge
6. Bridge Hill

7. White Hill
8. Georges Bay Rd
9. Evans Bay
10. Franks Bay
11. Church Road
12. Black Bay

13. Lighthouse
14. Riddells Bay
15. Khyber Pass
16. Belmont Manor
17. Cobbs Hill
18. Ord Road

19. Elbow Beach
20. Rural Hill
21. Hospital
22. Middle Rd
23. Hamilton Terminus
24. Richmond Rd

2. The Western Route of the Bermuda Railway

Tie-Tamping Near Elbow Beach Road
10-4-'31

Bermuda Archives

3. Tie-Tamping near Elbow Beach — 10th. April 1931

4. Construction work at Franks' Bay — circa April 1931

Bermuda Archives

5. The newly completed Somerset Railway Bridge — September 1931

Bermuda Archives

6. Tracks alongside West Main Road, near Church Road — June 1927 (?)

7. Recently completed trestle near Somerset drawbridge — June 1927

8. Governor cutting the ribbon at Somerset Bridge, 31st. October 1931

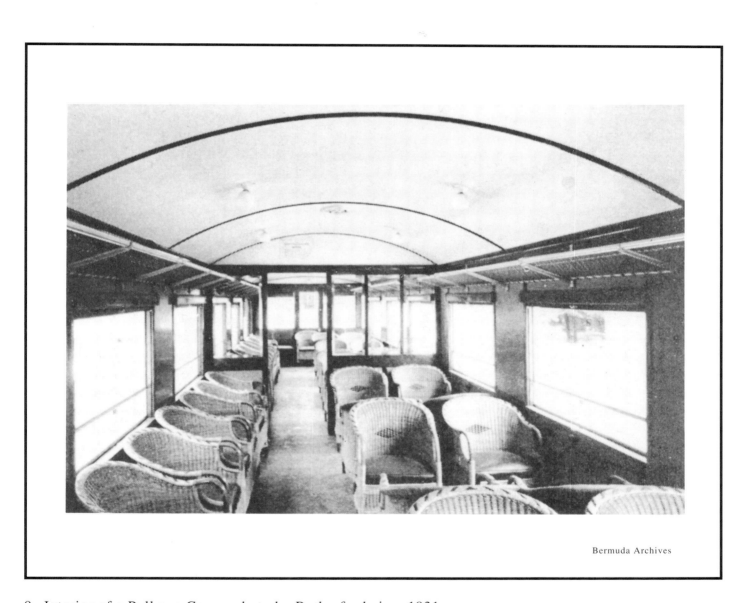

Bermuda Archives

9. Interior of a Pullman Car — photo by Rutherford circa 1931

Under the terms of the initial Railway Act of 1924, the company was approved as a business entity on the petition of Robert Augustus Cummings, identified as a businessman acting on behalf of the principal financial backers. It had already been estimated that close to half-a-million pounds might be required for the venture and the bulk of this money was to come from coordinated British banking circles. The Act allowed for this total investment to be divided into individual shares of ten pounds each.

Under the provisions of the 1924 Act, a Board of Directors was to be elected by the shareholders as soon as 50,000 pounds had been subscribed and the Governor was required to establish a special group of Railway Commissioners to serve as monitoring agents on behalf of the Government. Land acquisitions were to be made through the Commissioners and their tasks were also to include overseeing each ongoing phase of construction.

From this moment onwards, however, the development of a railway service for Bermuda seemed to be dogged by a host of problems and, almost inevitably, there were countless delays. Stipulations such as the track gauge (not to exceed 4'8 1/2") and the eventual requirement of 3 to 6 passenger trains per day, were not difficult to accommodate. Similarly, it was easy to satisfy Section 36, which required separate compartments for First and Second Class passengers, and it was just as simple to ensure that trains would travel no faster than 20 miles per hour. The company's economic advisors even seemed comfortable that their projected fare structures would be well within the official demands that children under the age of 3 should travel free, and that tickets should not exceed 3d. for those travelling in excess of five miles. However, other conditions proved to be far harder to comply with. One particularly awkward clause required the company to commence construction within 6 months of the final plan being granted approval; from a practical point of view, it proved absolutely impossible to adhere to this demand.

Prior to any ground breaking, the 'Railway Act, 1925' required that a detailed survey be made of the proposed route and the plan had to be presented to the Governor. The plan was to be on scale not less than 6 inches to the mile and had to be accompanied by supporting information, such as the results of any soil sampling or rock tests which may have been conducted. The Bermuda Government proved to be exceptionally thorough in studying every piece of information which the company presented; indeed, even the proposer of the Act, Mr. H. W. Watlington, could not have anticipated this degree of meticulous evaluation. Each item was scrutinized with such caution that on 19th. December 1927 — a full three years after the passing of the first piece of railway legislation — another 'Railway Company Act' had to be passed, extending the period originally specified for the actual start of construction. By 22nd. June 1929, still further legislation was required in order to extend the construction period even more. Then again, in June 1930, additional major delays were caused when the Government announced that it had decided to convert the Pemboke East Marsh into a recreation area. The entire section of railway in that vicinity, therefore, had to be totally redesigned along a completely different route.

In distant England, the backers of the scheme were isolated from the specific causes of daily obstacles which the company seemed to be facing; perhaps, on the other hand, they surmised that the unending succession of delays was the direct product of deliberate tactics adopted by lingering pockets of anti-railway resistance. However, this was certainly not the case. Even the most ardent advocates of the motor car had endorsed the railway and the attitude of many opponents was summed up by the Honourable S. S. Spurling, when he proclaimed to the House of Assembly, on Monday 7th. December 1925: "I am not able to see in any way how the railway is going to afford the transportation that Bermuda needs. But I also feel that if it is to be built at all then I shall do everything I can to make it as successful an enterprise as it can be made." So supportive did he become that later, as a Common Councillor on the Corporation of St. George, on 11th. July 1928, Stanley Spurling proposed that: "the railway project has matured to such an extent that the building and operation of the railway will be accomplished facts in the near future, and that the Corporation will be glad to confer with officials of the Railway Company with regard to the route and other matters of mutual advantage."

There never was any conspiracy to delay the railway's construction. Parliamentarians John Bluck, J. Reginald Conyers and F. Goodwin Gosling soon became shareholders and Mr. Spurling himself subsequently became a Director of the 'Bermuda Railway Company'.

On the contrary, the labourious rate of progress in laying the train track was the unavoidable outgrowth of such natural impediments as haggling over land acquisitions, non-arrival of building materials and such genuinely unpredictable obstacles as hard rock nodules outcropping in the centre of an embankment.

The spirit pervading the country was supportive of the railway and Bermudians felt generally optimistic about their economic future. Probably nowhere was that spirit — and the role of the railway in making that a reality — better epitomized than in Bermuda's oldest settlement and original capital, St. George. Fully aware that it stood to reap considerable benefits not only from the railway but also from the resort hotels and golf links being built at Mid Ocean and Castle Harbour, the town's elders banded together to work for the common good.

Corporation Secretary P. L. Lightbourne was in constant contact with staff at the offices of the 'Bermuda Railway Company' on Chancery Hill, in Hamilton, and expressed the collective view that the Corporation and the Company should hold regular meetings in order to resolve any problems which might arise. During the latter years of the 1920's decade, they convened to discuss ways of handling the extra volume of freight which would be off-loaded at the Tiger Bay dock and wharves; they considered how to speed the movement of disembarking steamship passengers from the docks and debated ways of dovetailing train and ferry schedules so as to avoid any congestion between people, animals, bicycles and carriages.

But even with this generous desire for unequivocal cooperation, countless creases still needed to be ironed-out. In October 1928, the cash sensitive Railway Company requested, but was denied, a reduction in the levy of one shilling per ton, imposed by the St.

George's Corporation on all railway materials deposited on the wharf. In 1929, the two parties met to determine the specifics of the most appropriate route for the train to take into the St. George terminus; but, as had happened frequently across the country, this caused a variety of temporary delays whilst documented ownership was established on property adjacent to the local Grammar School, and along Stile Hill. Even as late as 20th. March 1931, the old Corporation found itself having to negotiate the willingness of Messrs. J. D. C. Darrell and William E. Meyer to sell portions of Hunters Wharf, so that extra tracks might be laid down between the new dock and the area north of Penno's Wharf. A committee comprised of Leon Fox, R. C. McAllan and S. S. Spurling was appointed to investigate the matter.

For the railway's financiers, developers, designers and workers, this succession of minor delays was undoubtedly frustrating. But they were unavoidable nevertheless. Nobody was erecting deliberate obstacles. Rather, ever since 1924, public excitement had continued to grow steadily towards a crescendo as Bermudians awaited that novel experience of the first joy ride.

Convinced that all forms of modernisation had to be embraced by these tranquil islands, the ebullient St. George's Councillor Mr. H. L. Ingham characterized the country's excited mood by announcing to his constituents that he had researched an entirely revolutionary method of street cleaning, one which involved attaching a circular broom to a moving motor lorry. He proposed that Mayor W. J. Boyle should order one straightaway from 'C. H. Hvass Co.' of New York, and then trumpetted his way along Water Street, proclaiming that such devices were the form of the future. In 1931, the town bought its first 30 cwt. Morris truck, and on 20th. August Mr. Harry Roberts was instructed to remove the ring bolts, traditionally used to tether horses, from the eastern wall of the Town Hall. Symbolically, St. George was on the verge of entering a new era of modern transportation.

Gradually, railway tracks spread all the way from Somerset to Hamilton. Bridges were erected over bays; embankments were cut into the sides of slopes. As an engineering device to avoid the exhorbitant costs and delays involved with land aquisitions, large stretches of track skirted the shoreline and were supported on wooden trestles. In all, a total of 33 were built between Mangrove Bay, in the western parish of Sandys, and Tiger Bay, in the east. Virtually all of the way from Shelly Bay through to Bailey's Bay, the railway line traced its way above the water and along the coastline parallel to the base of Crawl Hill cliffs. At Coney Island, it crossed concrete pillars over to Ferry Reach. With indominatable determination, the company's surveyors and engineers had confronted every apparent obstacle and treated each as no more than a challenge to their ingenuity. By October 1931, they confidently announced that they were about to open the full western half of the railway.

In contrast to the negative international press which had surrounded public railway services in 1924, the picture being painted in 1931 was significantly different. In England, the Great Western Railway proudly announced that its regular afternoon express train between Cheltenham and London had covered the distance in just 57 minutes, at the phenomenal speed of 69.2 miles per hour — the fastest passenger train in the world. Although speed was not a factor to be emulated in Bermuda, the local newspapers were enthusiastic in reporting that such speeds had been steadily increasing since 1914, when England's Stockton to York train had been timed at 61.7 m.p.h. In 1929, the Paris-St. Quentin express had attained 64.8 m.p.h. When the Canadians announced in 1930 that the Montreal-South Fall run of 124 miles had averaged 68.9 m.p.h., it was obvious that it would be just a matter of time before the British responded with something faster.

As Bermuda prepared to open its first railway in 1931, danger and accidents, evidently, had ceased to be a consideration for the public mind. In fact, that same year a story filtered its way along Front Street, with some degree of amusement, proclaiming that an eccentric Englishman had successfully defeated a racing pigeon in a race over a 150 mile course, during which he had used an automobile and a train. If railways had now entered the entertainment arena with this type of frivolity, then clearly there was very little for Bermudians to worry about! Meanwhile, the enterprising Canadians had discovered another advantage of railways; C. N. R. was sponsoring a 'soil improvement train' entitled "The Dominion Experimental Farm", which would travel out to remote farming areas offering valuable lectures on such topics as soil fertilization. Railways offered limitless prospects.

There was no doubt that trains were here to stay. Bermuda was becoming part of this world-wide revolution in mass transport.

4

Into the Age of Rail

Bermuda, by the mid 1920's, was becoming quite accustomed to the new ideas and inventions which were sweeping the world and Bermudians felt comfortable with themselves over how they had managed to accept all manner of innovations, with surprising ease.

Telephone poles had sprung up along sections of roadside and electric lighting was slowly creeping its way across the landscape; there was rumour of a plan to install night-time lighting on the wharves at Hamilton and St. George. Telegraphy cables were no longer viewed with suspicion. There was even a report, of course not completely verified nor believed, that one wireless enthusiast had actually sat listening to an English Broadcasting signal throughout most of the last Thursday of November 1925. That same year, it was by telegram that Bermuda speedily received news of the death of Her Majesty Queen Alexandra on 20th. November. At the Mechanics Hall, in Hamilton, the 'Humanophone Company' was showing a moving picture entitled 'Loves at Christmastime' starring Bebe Daniels and an actor named Harrison Ford.

Following the successful flight from London to Capetown by British aviator Alan Cobham in the middle of the decade, there was widespread talk that this form of transport could eventually become available for all. As Bermuda geared itself towards the future, there were those who could forecast the day when perhaps air travel might be used to carry visitors to these fair shores. It seemed that anything, in those days, was possible.

Adjusting to the prospects of a newly reorientated economy based on tourism, Government budgeted to undertake some major projects. These plans included the cleaning of Riddell's Bay and Salt Kettle; massive road improvements from Khyber Pass to Somerset and repairs to the bridge at Cavello Bay. In order to accommodate the larger cruise ships which were expected "in the foreseeable future", detailed surveys were made of potential channels which could be used to bring them into Hamilton. Down in St. George, work on the Town Cut had already been completed, but now marine engineers were already taking a fresh look at its adequacy. What a disaster if it couldn't handle the enormous vessels which were reputed to be leaving the drawing boards of European shipyards!

Among others in the House of Assembly, Major Thomas Dill, Mr. F. Goodwin Gosling, the Honourable H. W. Watlington, W. F. Perinchief, Mr. A. B. Smith and Stanley Spurling seemed always at the forefront of any debate which sought to turn the economic base of Bermuda onto this exciting, new trajectory. In some respects they represented a vocal vanguard in the quest to draw their country into the heart of the twentieth century. By 1926, a battery of legislation had been passed by the House of Assembly within just a few months. Significantly, each law, in one way or the other, sought to facilitate, promote and satisfy the countless dynamics of tourism. They included: 'The Aquarium Act', 'The Bermuda Hotel Act', 'The Dredging Act', The Smoke Shop Act', 'The Hospital Act', 'The Telegraphy Wireless and Signalling Act', 'Refuse Disposal Act' and 'The Liquor Control Act'. The offices of Colonial Secretary H. Henniker Heaton hummed with perpetual activity.

The railway concept, however, still had its active opponents and on 2nd. December 1925, the Government received a letter from one such group demanding that a plebicite be held so that the entire population might have a say in whether or not there should be trains in Bermuda. Their argument, in part, proposed that tourism would effectively suffer as a result of visitors seeing the country far too quickly and that coastal damage would be so extensive that it would distract from the islands' natural beauty. Soberly, the newspaper reported that the rail service in Britain had nearly been brought to a standstill, as a result of a strike by its employees, over salaries and redundancies. Work disruptions and strikes in Bermuda? Perish the thought!

Even in the House, support was far from unanimous and when the 'Bermuda Railway Act No. 2' came up for a first reading a few days before the end of 1925, parliamentarian W. A. Moore defiantly called for the introduction of "a proper horse bus service'. Mr. H. V. Smith blandly commented that the Jamaica Railway had failed. Fellow member Mr. T. H. H. Outerbridge complained that "commercial conscience" should not permit a company to invest "200,000 pounds in something which they knew would never pay". Mr. Conyers pointed out that Bermuda did not have the financial reserves to back a failure. However, by that stage, a majority was committed to the idea and Sir Reginald Gray proposed that surveying work should go ahead within 5 months of the Act becoming law. Supporting colleagues voted that the railway should proceed without further unwarranted disruptions.

By 12th. June 1930, a total of six individual Acts had been scrutinized by the Legislature on behalf of the 'Bermuda Railway Company'. Progressively, they had sought to incoporate the company, provide it with safeguards from competition and define its objectives. Special clauses were inserted to stipulate definite conditions to be met when applying to acquire property deemed essential to the previously approved route. Other amendments covered procedures for planning the actual route, taking geological samples and making soil tests. Several development schedules were prepared and revised, and each time, Mr. O. A. Jones, principal field director for the project's construction agents — 'Balfour, Beatty & Co.Ltd.' — patiently undertook to reorganise his work force, yet again.

Progress was slow, but steady. Bridges began to appear at Coney Island, at Flatts and up in Somerset; small sub-stations were built at Prospect Garrison, all along Middle Road in Paget and at the West India Company Oil docks on Ferry Reach. Space was allocated for three stops along Ord Road, and others were planned at Government House, Shelly Bay, Richmond Road, Serpentine Road, Khyber Pass, Belmont Manor, Church Bay .... in fact, provisions were made so that virtually everywhere from Mullet Bay through to Mangrove Bay would be accessible to the railway. In all, 42 stops were projected and the area around each halt had to be cleared and prepared to receive passengers, trains and track. In between, land had been reclaimed, hillsides were sliced into embankments and flat bedding was readied to receive lengths of rail. At a meeting with concerned citizens of Somerset, in October 1931, Frank Stemp, general manager of the 'Bermuda Railway Company', assured his audience that the company was determined to serve the public — and if they needed shelters for their cycles, then shelters they would get! With impressive haste, free storage for 50 bicycles was provided. More expenses; more delays.

There were, of course, many delays but none exceeded the drastic, last minute upheaval of having to replan a complete section of track formerly surveyed to pass along the northern corner of Pembroke Parish, just where it turned southwards into the City of Hamilton. In early 1931, an embarrassed Public Works Department suddenly discovered that the approved railway route would directly interfere with its own intention, also approved, to develop a small part of Pembroke Marsh, as a community recreation centre. (Later known as Barnard Park.) Without choice, therefore, the Railway Company was obliged to landscape an alternative route, one which skirted the marsh and involved excavating a small tunnel beneath the roadway close to St. John's Church. In consequence of this strange turn of events, the Chairman of the Commissioners, Mr. R. W. Appleby, informed the Government in a letter dated 7th. August 1931, that the extra work and acquisition of new land had cost the company 7,115 pounds as opposed to the original estimate of 3,850 pounds.

Having been forced to deviate from their original plans, the company raised the question of complete reimbursement in the House of Assembly, a request which the Government agreed to accept in full. There was, however, no apology for this inexcusable faux pas and the company bore the full brunt of the inconvenience. Instead of acquiring 1.335 acres of land from Saltus Grammar School, Bermuda Amateur Athletic Association, John James, Clara Walker and L. R. Motyer, individual deals had to be hastily negotiated to secure a total of 1.3544 acres from an entirely different group of individuals, including: Messrs. Lambe, Sheppard, Jackson, J. H. Taylor, Samuel Smith, T. M. Dill, Eldred Smith, Aubrey Robinson, Mrs. A. Richardson, Mrs. Walker, Mrs. F. W. Joell and the Motyer family. For his trouble and cooperation, Mr. W. E. P. Motyer ended up with a so-called 'Life Pass' for the railway, valued at 200 pounds.

As gangster Al Capone prepared to go on trial in Chicago on 7th. October 1931, Dr. William Beebee addressed Bermudian Rotarians on the subject of "Fear and Exploration". Outside the Hamilton hotel, railway workers were busy cutting a route into the city; and visiting expert Mr. Stansbury, of 'The Philadelphia Bitrodite Paving Company' was preparing the specifics of a plan to upgrade streets, to meet the demands of increasing traffic. On Front Street, 'Wadsons' was busy promoting bicycles as the best way "to dodge in and out of traffic, your creditors, the high cost of living and sometime perhaps the railway!"

In England, Flight Lieutenant G. H. Stainforth, according to the 'Science Christian Monitor', had flown a 3 kilometer course at the impossible speed of 388.67 m.p.h. and there were warnings that "the airplane justifies its existence only by the things which make it superior to other methods of transportation. Speed is no idle sporting preparation; no question of thrill seeking." In far away Japan, motor tricycles were being mooted as the best way to encourage tourists to see all of Tokyo. As Bermuda hesitatingly took its first steps into modern mass transport, other nations were seemingly preparing to enter another.

As the completion date approached, the first full trial run was made from Hamilton to Somerset during the afternoon of Tuesday 13th. October 1931. Among the select group of a dozen invited passengers was a reporter from the 'Gazette', who was particularly impressed by the dual absence of noise and smoke — characteristics of train journeys in most other countries, especially when windows kept wide open. It was a journey, he commented, which offered the most delightful scenery in the shortest possible time: "the traveller is treated to a totally new conception of the magnificent views," he effused. Another person in that inaugural group was Harold Kitchen, the man who not only held the patent for the driving gear, but also had designed the passenger cars. The journey was competed in 44 minutes and was acclaimed faultless by those who made the trip.

Clearly satisfied with the results of the trial run, traffic manager Mr. Stemp confidently announced that he anticipated starting a regular passenger service on 1st. November, the day after its official opening. He said that he expected trains to run every half-hour; and, depending on demand, this might be increased to one every fifteen minutes. Including stops, the company projected that a normal run from Hamilton to Somerset would take roughly 55 minutes. The cost of a regular, single second class fare would be 1/9d.

On Wednesday 21st. October 1931, Mr. J. W. Cox chaired a session of the House of Assembly which agreed to allocate an additional 400 pounds for the Railway Commissioners' budget; this unforeseen expense was to cover the costs of having the Director of Public Works, Mr. W. Livingston, employed to inspect the permanent way, the bridges and trestles of the railroad. Captain Larg had been retained by the Commissioners to conduct similar inspections of the rolling stock, some more of which had just arrived from England aboard the steamship 'Bolivian', on Monday 20th. October. Captain Larg's first task was to check that the five coaches were undamaged from their rough crossing; they each received a clean bill of health, with extra praise for the smart crest painted on their sides.

With an almost perceptible sigh of relief, 'The Royal Gazette and Colonist Daily' finally announced on 28th. October 1931, that the railway would be officially opened on Saturday 31st. October by Governor Lt. General Sir Thomas Astley-Cubitt, at the new bridge in Somerset; symbolically, a young lady named Miss Grissell would drive in the last spike at the terminal immediately before the ribbon-cutting ceremony. On the following day, a Sunday, various church services would be held.. The announcement produced an excited wave of anticipation throughout the islands and, in an instant, the disappointments and endless delays were all forgotten; copies of the newspaper were quickly sold out as an eager public swarmed around news vendors and street sellers in search of details.

The opening of the Bermuda Railway went without a hitch. The official party assembled at Number One shed on Front Street, in Hamilton, where they were welcomed by a reception committee. First to greet Governor and Lady Cubit were Mr. & Mrs. O. A. Jones, manager for the contruction engineers, and the Honourable H.W.Waltington, who had guided most of the railway legislation through Parliament. Next in line came Mr.W.E.Stemp, managing director and traffic ordinator of the 'Bermuda Railway Company', and Mr.J.R.Conyers, Vice President of the company; then came Major R.W.Appleby, the Attorney General of Bermuda and one of the Railway Commissioners. Sir Thomas paused to chat with each man, then, followed by his aide-de-camp Lord Carew, he proceeded along the reception line to speak with Railway Commissioner Mr.G.S.Patton and other dignitaries who had assembled for this auspicious occasion.

Mr. Conyers then made a formal speech outlining the waxing and waning of events which had occurred during the seven years preceding this momentous event. Less sonorously, he mentioned that the Hamilton to St. George section would hopefully be completed very soon. After this, the guests mounted the awaiting train, Lady Cubitt pressed the electric starter button and, with a toot on the whistle and a gush of air from the brakes, they gently moved away. The driver that day was Mr. W. G. Amos. Travelling well on schedule, the train wound its way through the countryside and safely pulled to a halt at Somerset Bridge. At this point, they were greeted by the contractors' chief engineer Mr. Henry Clarke. His wife then handed the final spike to the Governor's step-daughter, who ceremoniously hammered it into place; hers was the last act in linking the entire western portion of the railway.

Several more speeches were then made. J. H. P. Patterson, Sandys Parish M.P., gave words of welcome to the Governor and his party, adding that he hoped that the railway would prove to be the long lost solution to Bermuda's complicated transport problems. Speaking on behalf construction engineers 'Balfour, Beatty and Company', Mr. O. A. Jones noted that the arrival of an operating railway in Bermuda was of equal importance as the development of hotels and the expansion of shipping services — together, each was working to the same common goal of enabling people to see and enjoy the beauty of Bermuda.

After a buffet reception at the Somerset terminal, the party returned to their seats on the train and proceeded back to Hamilton, accompanied by cheers and applause from the crowds which lined the route — and serenaded by the charming music of the 'Sammy Robbins Band'. As a precaution against accidents occurring during this tradition-breaking event, the train was preceded in each direction by an outrider driving a 'motor-speeder'. They reached Hamilton at 6.45 p.m., fifteen minutes behind schedule, mainly because of a fault to the air brakes in one carriage, which consequently was left at Riddell's Bay. Other than that, the return trip passed without any further hitches and when the party finally disembarked on Front Street, everyone agreed that they were impressed by the comfort of the ride and exhilarated by the wonderful scenic panoramas which changed with each twist of the track.

By and large, the day's proceedings had gone virtually to perfection. Bermuda now had an operating railway system — at least, half of one — and the company was confidently able to assure the general public that a regular schedule would commence the very next day and that a freight service would be functioning by the end of that week.

The following day, still buoyed by a sense of excitement and involvement, Governor Cubitt was given a tour of the tunnel being cut close to the Bermudiana Hotel, in Hamilton. Although railways were hardly a new experience for the well-travelled Sir Thomas Cubitt, he showed genuine interest in the engineering aspects of the work and listened most carefully as he was guided into the difficult tunnel section by works manager Mr. H. Clark and Captain Ross Winter.

That same Sunday, way up in Southampton, the 'Bermuda Railway Company' recorded its first fatality. Former parliamentarian Captain George Watts Hill Kempe had just finished his first ride on the train and, accompanied by his wife, carefully alighted at the stop at

Church Road. In the darkness, however, he lost his footing and fell over the edge of an embankment. Severely injured by the seven foot fall, Captain Kempe died from shock and concussion soon afterwards. A funeral service was held on Monday 2nd. November and an inquest was held in Southampton eight days later. In delivering his verdict, acting-coroner Mr. A. C. Smith absolved the company of any culpable blame for the sad tragedy, but made it quite clear that there was an obvious need to introduce some form of lighting and safety fences at all railway stations.

The recommendation was the first of many suggestions which would find their way into the Company's offices in Hamilton.

For the next seventeen years of its operation, the railway was constantly being fine-tuned. On that monumental opening day, the construction firm of 'Balfour, Beatty & Co.' had formally handed over the completed railway line to its rightful owners. Along with the rolling stock and train tracks, however, it had also surrendered its contractual obligations towards the project. From that moment onwards, the 'Bermuda Railway Company' assumed full and sole responsibility for the railway system. It would prove to be an onerous undertaking indeed.

10. Train passing along Front Street, Hamilton — photo by R. Surry April 1932

Bermuda Archives

11. Train crossing water at Bailey's Bay — photo by Rutherford c. 1933

Bermuda Archives

12. Passengers arriving at Bailey's Bay Station — photo by Knudson c. 1935

13. On-board ticket collector serving passengers — photo by Vilzak 1938

Bermuda Archives

14. Anatole Vilzak's ballet troup alighten at Shelly Bay Station — 1938

15. View of Flatts from the train — photo by Rutherford c.1933

Bermuda embraced modern transport with genuine warmth and showed every willingness to give its maximum support. The Trade Development Board, whose responsibilities included tourism, announced that its new advertising campaign had been redesigned to incorporate extensive promotion of new inland travelling convenience and sightseeing trips. The Corporation of St. George eagerly agreed to place an advertisement in the railway company's own brochure. Out at 'The Sunnyside Hotel' in Somerset, Manager William Madder had already released adverts which referred to its location near Carvello Bay, with "railway service only one block from the hotel." On 28th. November 1931, the new $8 million "Monarch of Bermuda", flagship of the 'Furness-Bermuda Line', left New York on her maiden voyage to Bermuda.

Railways, worldwide, were enjoying immense popularity. In Canada, 'The Grand Trunk Railway' was celebrating the 75th. anniversary of its route from Toronto to Montreal (opened in 1856). In England, 'The Railway Savings Bank' declared that, as of September 1931, deposits amounted 18 million pounds — an impressive and remarkably healthy sum for such a small independent corporation, particularly when compared to the 284 million pounds held by the Government's Post Office Savings Account.

From the outset, the 'Bermuda Railway Company' was aware that it had made a major commitment to serving the public. Although, naturally enough, the shareholders were expecting dividends on their respective investments, they had never been deceived into believing that this was like those 'get rich quick' schemes, used to lure capital into the Yukon and California. The Management recognized its responsibilities and, from the very beginning, the company adopted a policy which sought to address customers' needs as soon as they arose.

Hence, within a week of opening, an extra train was provided on the stretch from Somerset to Hamilton, so that prospective patrons could attend a gala performance of "Patience", at the Colonial Opera House. It was timed to depart from the West End on Wednesday 4th. November at 6.40 p.m., returning at 11.15 p.m.; an all inclusive return fare of 8 shillings was offered. A couple of days later, news came from the Reid Street Head Office that special weekly zone tickets would be issued, enabling regular First Class travellers to ride the whole western section with a single pass, for just one guinea; Second Class passengers could buy passes for 17/6d.

After one month of operations, management also made several minor adjustments to the published timetable, so as to provide passengers with regular trains when they were most in demand. The very first public train had run on Sunday 1st. November, leaving Hamilton just after 6 a.m. But with only one passenger for much of the way, this was instantly abandoned! Similarly, it was discovered next that there was little or no call for a Somerset departure at 6.25 a.m. — although, oddly enough, the earlier one leaving Somerset at 5.50 a.m., and arriving in Hamilton at 6.54 a.m., was usually quite full. Also discontinued within those first four weeks was the 5.24 a.m. from Hamilton, which proved to have virtually no demand whatsoever. In short, the company was starting to gain a more sophisticated understanding of the demographic movement of Bermudians, particularly as they journeyed to and from work: some went to Hamilton each day to work in offices, or guest houses; others worked on the docks. Each group, however, did not necessarily travel at the same time, nor from the same stations. Likewise, farm labourers tended to be short-distance travellers, hopping on the train and then getting off just a few stops further up the line. Shoppers were like tourists: they invariably travelled later in the day, more spontaneously and with less predictability. For each type of passenger, the needs were quite different.

These were embryonic days and controversy often surfaced, almost inevitably perhaps, without being courted. On several occasions the 'Bermuda Railway Company' found unwanted publicity, as the target of debate in the House of Assembly. In 1931, distressed at what he misinterpreted as discriminatory price structures which disadvantaged his constituents, Mr. F. C. Misick (M. P. for Southampton) complained that overcharging was occurring, in contravention of the terms of the 1924 Railway Act. In an open letter addressed to the editor of the newspaper, dated 11th. November 1931, General Manager F. R. Stemp clarified that the so-called "Workmen's Tickets" were intended for all regular passengers and, although they were indeed available only on very specific trains, they were not intended for just one segment of the work force. On another occasion, Stemp was obliged to concede that some conductors had inadvertently miscalculated occasional fares, particularly during the busy rush hours, but vehemently refuted accusations that there had been deliberate wrongdoing on behalf of any railway staff.

Such misunderstandings, of course, were little more than teething troubles and, on the whole, the railway entered the daily lives of Bermudians with well-oiled ease. Certainly there had been absolutely nothing to approach the scale of confusion generated by the timetabling of the earliest Canadian trains — when different time-zones had been completely overlooked and all arrivals and departures were printed solely in Montreal time!

On Friday 13th. November 1931, the tunnel at Pitts Bay Road was blasted clear, paving the way for the Front Street tracks to become joined with their northern exit from Hamilton — and therefore enabling the eastern section of track from St. George to be finally integrated into the network. Mrs. Jones, wife of the construction manager, set off the last charge inside the tunnel and daylight miraculously shone through a small hole from either end. She was applauded by a dust showered crowd of onlookers and given a bouquet by Superintendent W. N. T. Williams; he then turned to commend the efforts of engineers Mr. H. Clarke and Mr. T. C. Claude and their army of workers, all of whom had laboured loyally in the heat since late summer.

The delays in integrating the St. George's portion of track into the rest, were not due exclusively to the Pitts Bay tunnel. On the contrary, that aspect of the work had been accomplished within the impressive period of just eight weeks. Many of the delays had been caused elsewhere, forming a string of events and complications which came to characterize the ongoing problems faced by the Railway Company; problems which would continue to plague it throughout its existence.

There proved to be far more to the day-to-day operating of a railway than just selling tickets, maintaining the rolling stock and pleasing travellers.

There were questions, for example, of lighting: who should pay the electricity bills and should parishes be responsible for providing or erecting their own light poles? There were issues such as the provision of parking facilities for passengers bicycles at smaller halts, and discussions on whether to offer restaurant services at major stations. All of these things, and others it seemed, fell within the domain of railway officials. In September 1932, for example, Managing Director Stemp wrote to the Corporation of St. George on behalf of the 'Bermuda Railway Company', requesting approval to sub-let an end section of railway-leased property to Messrs. W. Frith and E. Williams, who were keen to operate a small restaurant and bar at the St. George terminal. Not sure that he really wanted, in the first place, to get involved with someone else's desire to serve tea and scones to waiting railway passengers, Mr. Stemp nevertheless spent a lot of valuable time dealing with this matter — only to have it initially rejected by a Streets Committee "not favourably disposed towards this proposal." (Shortly afterwards, Corporation member Leon Fox was granted permission to lease his 'Sunnybank' wharf front property to Nicholas Callabras — to open a convenience store near the station.)

In a similar vein, Stemp also became involved with petitioning a request on behalf of 'The Society for the Prevention of Cruelty to Animals', whose Secretary, Mr. Frank E. Gurr, had been previously refused approval to erect water troughs for horses at various railway stations. On 18th. January 1933, the already over-extended Mr. Stemp was approached by East End hoteliers, requesting the provision of trains to meet Charlie Christianson's ferry service across Castle Harbour; they also expected Stemp to advertise the schedule as soon as the logistics had been resolved. On top of this came an application from the Northumberland Fusiliers, who wondered whether their band could get a special inclusive rate when it travelled for performances during upcoming 'Somers Day' celebrations.

In addition to these necessary distractions, the company also had to concentrate on its own, very real priority items: wharfage fees, fuel taxes, insurance policies, fuel storage sheds, staffing, wages and rents. There were always unavoidable meetings to attend, such as those required to renegotiate the lease of land and buildings at Penno's Wharf — property which the 'Bermuda Railway Company' had leased since 4th. October 1924, but which Corporation lawyers 'Gray and Smith' now felt required reviewing after seven years. (The outcome, in 1932, was a reduction in rent, the demolition of one cottage and the conversion of another into stores and staff sleeping quarters.) There were discussions, too, with the Board of Agriculture, concerning the provision of cold-storage facilities for freshly landed freight, as well as that produce being moved internally.

The legal repercussions of various land purchases likewise simmered for several years. Eventually, all property dossiers were handed over to a congenial employee named Mr. Blee, who was delegated to resolve all real estate matters for the 'Bermuda Railway Company'. His was an awesome, unenviable task.

After two years, the affable Mr. Blee was still patiently trying to effect the transfer of a solitary narrow strip of land described as "the old road south of the tracks at Tiger Bay", to the St. George Corporation, in lieu of another piece referred to as "the new road"; all of which was complicated by virtue of the company having originally bought an adjacent piece of property from the War Department, in London. At some point, everyone would get their just desserts — including nearby householders, who wanted assurances that they would be able to have safe access to their own property across the tracks. Obviously, this was a sensitive job; one involving a peculiar blend of diplomacy and arm-wrestling when he met with lawyers, Aldermen, Mayor Meyer, Councillors, landowners, engineers and 'Bermuda Railway Company' representatives. Every one of them desperately hoped that the kindly Mr. Blee would not suffer inopportune burnout before the delicate intricacies of these and other cases were resolved!

In the interim, when the Honourable J. P. Hand secured a regular service between Boston and Bermuda, it was Mr. Stemp who conferred with Captain Armett of the 'Canadian National Steamship Company' over the availability of additional freight space on the docks. 'C. N. S.' General Manager A. H. Allen liased regularly with the railway company, seeking to ensure extra trains to meet the ships. Business of this nature was a daily digression for the growing staff at the company's Reid Street headquarters: as one person arranged for the sale of surplus embankment fill, another met with Chief Engineer Harold Kitchen to evaluate the performance of engines, the adequacy of compartments and the general comfort of passengers. Another staffer, meanwhile, attended meetings with carriage drivers, hoping to resolve complaints that trains represented unfair competition to their own business. They were all very busy.

In 1933, some relief emerged when the Honourable S. S. Spurling was elected to the office of Alderman on the Corporation of St. George. As a Director of the 'Bermuda Railway Company', he became the chief link between the company and the town; the conduit for information and decisions between Hamilton and the East End. It was he who handled the potentially explosive issue of limiting gasoline storage to a mere 50 barrels at a time, and requests for a train to meet the fifteen minute ferry service over to 'Castle Harbour Hotel'. On his shoulders fell the burden of resolving poor drainage in the goods shed, the provision of an alternative passenger entrance at the terminal, and the thorny issue of traffic congestion at Tiger Bay, which occurred when everyone converged simultaneously to meet the ships. That year, it was Spurling who negotiated arrangements for 'Messrs. K. A. Lasley Inc.' of New York to conduct a tourism survey; and it was Stanley Spurling who aways sat with the Chamber of Commerce to discuss the diverse topics of mutual concern which arose from the rapidly expanding tourist trade. In June 1934, he was knighted by King George.

By cultivating direct contacts with these and other organizations, as well as supporting the activities of the recently created 'Bermuda News Bureau', the railway's decision-makers secured instant access to the pulse of the country's needs. This insight enabled them to anticipate changes, allowing the company to predict future requirements and obligations.

Certainly, in Bermuda's future, a place had to be reserved for the automobile and, in readiness of such an eventuality, the House of Assembly passed 'The Motor Car Act

1934'. Whereas previous legislation typically focused on types of vehicles and definitions of technical words, this particular law required that all mechanized transport, and their drivers, must have individual licenses. Traffic Ordinances were likewise placed under review and opinions were solicited from the police in order to formulate an all-encompassing policy to regulate increases in all categories of automobiles — from steamrollers, to lorries and cars. An engineer, Lawrence H. Smith, was retained by the Government to assist in planning better roads throughout the islands.

There was, of course, no way to measure the impact of alternative mechanical modes of travel, on the railway. Vehicle numbers were far too small and none were designed to compete with Bermuda's only existing system of mass transport. Passenger and freight returns merely served to confirm that 'The Bermuda Railway Company' was continuing to serve the community effectively, and that the general public was supporting it wholeheartedly. There were advertisements in all of the favourite guidebooks and "Bushell's Handbook" not only made reference to fares and schedules, but even included a map of the route. In 1935, author Carveth Wells devoted an entire chapter in his book "Bermuda in Three Colours" to describing the wonders to be experienced during a train ride from Hamilton to Somerset. That same year, King Edward VIII ascended to the British throne and Bermuda looked forward to celebrating the November coronation. In 1936, the railway was featured in "Bermudiana", a photographic essay compiled by R. J. Williams.

Author Carveth Wells, was truly enchanted by his train ride from Hamilton to Somerset and he wrote expansively about the spectacular views which passengers should expect throughout the trip. Consequently, his book became a leading source of free publicity for the railway. His American publishers must also have been equally as charmed by it, for they overcame all manner of technical complications to include a map of the railway on the inside of the book's dust jacket.

Without a shadow of doubt, the Bermuda railway had succeeded in establishing itself as a major tourist attraction, as well as an essential means of travel for all who lived here. The company even received an official letter of commendation, thanking it for the significant contribution which the railway had made towards the development of tourism in St. George — and a request that railway engineers look into the costs of extending the tracks directly into King's Square.

From all outward signs, the 'Bermuda Railway Company' had been an outstanding success. However, neither the compliments nor support had ever translated themselves into healthy monetary returns and when the Board of Directors convened in 1938, they expressed the deepening worries harboured by all shareholders. If the company was on viable financial footing, why had it continuously felt obliged to apply for annual municipal and parochial tax relief? Had any aspect of the company's financial woes been reversed since 28th. October 1936, when Secretary W. J. Curtis reported: "The company's earnings are not sufficient to meet claims of interest on the loan capital, including debentures received. It is not possible to set aside any reserves whatsoever."

The answers to these and other questions emerged as no less discouraging. Wearily, the Secretary explained that a considerable amount of equipment had depreciated and some rolling stock was already obsolete; whatever profits were being made, therefore, needed to be injected straight back into maintenance and renewals. There was, however, still a deep sense of commitment towards serving the country and the meeting adjourned with agreement to release the optimistic message that: "the Company feels that the continued operation of the railway is of vital interest to the welfare of Bermuda — and benefits allowed to the Company will benefit the country."

This upbeat mood in Hamilton, however, did not translate itself into special treatment in the market place. Rents still had to be paid; fuel had to bought and tracks had to be checked. In October 1938, there was a demand that proper flushing toilets be installed at all main terminals. In the pressing interests of public health, company accountants sifted through finances looking for a way to budget for this expenditure. Two other woesome signals also flickered at about this same time. On 2nd. February 1939, the Corporation of St. George announced that, due to a shortage of funds, it was unable to advertise in the 'B. R. Co.' booklet; this represented one small but additional loss of revenue. Secondly, in what many interpreted to be a symbolic defection of support, 'Spurling Brothers' applied to the planning authorities for permission to build a bridge over York Street, "for motor vehicles".

As the world tottered on the edge of war, it was starting to look as if the era of the railway in Bermuda was about to be eclipsed. In December 1939, letters went out to creditors asking for extensions on invoices and reductions in rents. By then, Austria and Czechoslovakia had already fallen and Churchill's darkest days lay ahead.

6

The War Years

As the early morning train from Somerset to Hamilton rumbled its way across the trestles at Frank's Bay and headed towards the upcoming station at Church Road in Southampton, rumbles of an entirely different nature were quaking the mountains and farmlands of Europe. In the autumn of 1939, Britain's ultimatum for peace with Germany expired; another world war was declared.

The impact of the war on Bermuda's railway was both a blessing, and a disaster. In one respect, the presence of troops on these islands was of unquestionable benefit to the economy. Soldiers and sailors needed to eat and drink, and they seemed quite content to venture from the docks and their barracks in search of both. The seamen usually came for brief spells of shore leave; seeking land bound refuge from the notorious 'U' boats which were known to be prowling the waters of the North Atlantic. Soldiers usually came to reinforce or replace the forces already billeted on these shores; they were stationed mainly at the barracks in Prospect and St. George but, like their naval colleagues, could be found all over the country. Convoys passed along the coast, sometimes coming through the reefs and into the harbours in order to regroup and refuel.

Whatever the reasons, there was a significant increase of the military presence in Bermuda throughout the war years, and this resulted in a decidedly greater number of passengers using the railway. Ironically, although each travelling serviceman represented another paid ticket, all of which which added to the company's coffers, the sheer volume of these and regular passengers actually had an adverse effect on the railway — one which indirectly contributed to its collapse.

When author Carveth Wells had described his experiences on the train in 1935, he had seen it from the point of view of a tourist. Even in his revised edition of 1938, he still perceived the railway primarily as a means of enjoying the natural beauty of Bermuda; at worst, it was a wonderful way to go to work. With this in mind, he even suggested that passengers chose the righthand side of the compartment for the trip up to Somerset, since this afforded the most picturesque landscapes. He mentioned the masses of blue Morning Glories and scarlet Hibiscus at the Foot-of-the-Lane and the preponderance of red Lantana growing wild, around the edges of banana plantations at Rural Hill, in Paget. Along Ord Road, the railway offered glimpses of lily fields, strawberry gardens, palm trees and an abundance of pawpaws; there were fine palms everywhere and Poinsettias rising high above the rolling, green landscape of Belmont Manor, all the way out beyond Warwick and into Southampton Parish. Passed Riddell's Bay Station, he became more and more enthusiastic about the sights of little bays, Gibb's Hill lighthouse, the old wrecks of two forgotten naval ships and the sight of Spectacle and Heart Islands. At the Bridge Hill Stop, near Somerset Bridge, he was verily overcome by the sight of the multicoloured sea and the distant view of Cathedral rocks and its coral cliffs.

This, perhaps, conjured the real nature of the Bermuda railway. From the very inception of the idea, way back in the 1920's when 'Furness Withy' suggested the total development of tourism in Bermuda, it had indeed been intended to provide a means whereby residents and visitors would be able to travel around quickly and enjoy the scenery. To this end, even the interior of the carriages had been designed for genteel comfort, with wicker seats and wooden arm rests. Ladies in bonnets placed their shopping on small overhead racks; there was room for men to stretch their legs whilst reading the newspaper on the way home from work. Children sat in their own places or played on the floor, as older brothers and sisters peered through windows at the passing landscape. It was indeed custom built for these civilized needs.

What the railway was not designed for was the daily pounding of army boots along the aisles; the tossing and dropping of heavy rucksacks, or the incessant, accidental banging of rifle butts against wooden arm rests. If warships docked in Hamilton, then invariably there were men and equipment to be transferred to the St. George's barracks, or who needed billeting up at the Prospect Headquarters. The British army constantly used the local trains. There were nightly loads of off-duty soldiers making their way from Prospect down to Front Street, and, when they needed to return home several hours later, the Hamilton Terminal bustled with business such as it had never seen before. Likewise, hundreds of sailors regularly journeyed from the Royal Naval Dockyard in search of exciting nightlife all over Bermuda.

The situation at the St. George Terminal was no quieter. Indeed, after 1941, there was even more activity down at the East End. Following the signing of an agreement for the United States Government to build an airbase and submarine facility onto parts of St. David's and Longbird Islands, Bermuda's ancient capital bounced with unprecedented turmoil. Supplies and personnel arrived in the harbour and were off-loaded at the increasingly congested docks; labour and material which landed in Hamilton had to be trained down to St. George, and visa versa. And so it was that when highranking British and American officials concluded their famous 'Destroyer Deal' they were indirectly responsible for injecting yet another source of support, and burden, on the already overtaxed Bermuda railway system. Regrettably, with part of the island's work force fighting in the battlefields of Europe and North Africa, the railway company's own cleaning, servicing and maintenance staff consequently had been depleted drastically — at a time when, it transpired, they were needed desperately at home.

Certainly the armed forces were good customers and, for the duration of the war, they contributed a welcome bonanza of several thousand extra paying travellers on the trains each year. However, this was not without its drawbacks. When the carriage makers had customized the pullman cars for Bermuda, there had never been any special provision for this form of heavy duty wear and tear. Therefore, when general maintenance was already falling behind because of wartime staff shortages, the railway company's services were extended to and beyond the limit. Studded army boots wore into the wooden flooring faster than ladies' shoes; rifles resting across the seats inflicted more damage than an umbrella; the filled backpack of a man on his way to war, strained more heavily on the racks than bags of family shopping.

Ironically, therefore, this new volume of business inflicted unprecedented damage and strain on the company's already deteriorating rolling stock, at the point when it was less able to effect repairs. Also, spare parts were harder to acquire in the war years; British factories were commandeered for military purposes and shipping convoys had other priorities than the Bermuda railway's needs. Within just a few short years, the increased volume of passenger and freight traffic began to take its toll. The degree of comfort which Carveth Wells had applauded back in 1938, had, by 1941, deteriorated dramatically.

And so it was that the forces which once seemed to be converging for the railway's salvation, were now unwittingly proving to be conspirators in forging its doom.

This upsurge in user volume had other repercussions too, each of which further burdened the company's revenue. There were demands from Parish Councils and Government that toilet facilities should be improved at terminals and major stops. In St. George, the Corporation had repeatedly called for more urinals and a larger waste pit; by 1942, this had become a firm demand and threats of involving the Board of Health were made. Similarly, the constant use of streets and footpaths in the vicinity of the tracks was causing severe deterioration to road surfaces; ruts cut by wagon wheels and excavated by poor drainage meant that some sections of line were flooded and dangerous to cross after a heavy downpour. In turn, each of these problems was placed before the 'Bermuda Railway Company' and a growing list of priority issues sprawled its way over Frank Stemp's desk in the Managing Director's office.

Top level meetings were called throughout the war to examine each problem as it arose, in the hope of finding ready solutions. Progressively, however, these became harder to find. Tracks needed constant checking by road gangs; all rolling stock required daily maintenance; carriages needed to be kept clean and seats required repairing on a more regular basis. Normal usage necessitated overhauling of the railway engines and spare parts had to be kept on hand; a depleted engineering staff worked night and day to keep their charges on schedule, whilst harassed maintenance gangs were shuttled desperately from East to West, and back again. At Company Headquarters in Hamilton, Vice President J. Reginald Conyers looked around the room and struggled to solve the growing dilemma: John Bluck, Harry Butterfield, William J. Curtis, Joseph D. W. Darrell, Goodwin Gosling, Eldon H. Trimingham, Antoinette Lightbourn and Sir Stanley Spurling debated, argued and discussed. Frank Stemp and Harold Kitchen made suggestions. But none had a magic wand.

By 1945, revenue was failing to keep pace with the demands of operating expenses. The longer this dilemma persisted, the greater became the gulf between profits and losses. The narrower that margin became, so the company became less and less able to finance the major projects it had to undertake in order to overhaul and update the system. Unable to accomplish these, then inevitably the safety and effectiveness of the entire service was called into question.

The following year, the Bermuda Government bought the faltering company for the sum of 115,000 pounds. 'The Bermuda Railway Company' had been functioning in a state of dwindling helplessness and the Government seemed compromised into making the purchase, as a desperate bid to salvage the country's principal means of public transport. However, when it studied closely the firm's books, the general picture was far more distressing than had been appreciated. Not only was the rolling stock in dire need of attention, but so were bridges, trestles and lengths of rail. Dozens of sleepers required replacing everywhere. At this stage, there could have been little doubt that the future of the Bermuda Railway was decidedly bleak;

its days would be very, very limited in number.

Apparently, 21 miles of the most scenic railway in the World, and an estimated 14 million passengers during a 17 year period, were insufficient to keep it viable.

On hindsight, there was also one other aspect which had never been correctly addressed by the railway builders. The philosophy behind the scheme had always been to carry people rapidly from East to West, in a manner which would enable them to enjoy the scenery. Very much in mind, had always been the role which the railway needed to play in the development of tourism; this was particularly and unashamedly so when its opening coincided with major hotel construction in the late 1920's and early 1930's. The impetus, of course, had been largely due to the vision of 'Furness Withy' and much of the marketing strategy targeted tourists. Such an attitude, however, was not only naive but was also fatally restrictive, for it failed to recognize the need to court the wholehearted support of the country's permanent residents — and all of the residents, regardless of where they were living. A failure to have the railway accessible and convenient for everyone resulted in a large percentage of the population not using it on a regular basis; many used it once, as a novelty, and never rode it again.

Although the original investors expected the existence of an island-wide railway to be a service attractive to all Bermudians, the reality of it was that that the majority of the population rarely used it, if at all. For example, with the tracks cutting exclusively along the North Shore of Smiths and Devonshire Parishes, people living in the southern parts of those areas felt virtually disconnected from the railway as a public service. They didn't see it, rarely heard it and the inconvenience of having to either walk or catch a carriage to the nearest station reduced its appeal as a travel option. Unless they lived directly along the route, Hamilton's commuters continued to cycle just as they always had.

It is interesting to pay full attention to the casual reminiscences of Bermudians from that period and notice the prevailing marked absence of reference to the railway. Most St. David's Islanders, if they ever went to Hamilton at all, continued to use their boats; folk from Ireland and Watford Islands tended to stick with the ferries. Those with homes out at Tuckers Town, used their carriages; from Devil's Hole, they cycled. When reflecting on the development of his pioneering business, Easter Lily farmer Mr. Howard Smith, whose own extensive travels in North America had made him quite familiar with trains, made absolutely no references whatsoever to the Bermuda Railway. In Gilbert Butland's autobiography of 1986, he describes his life as teacher and headmaster at Whitney Institute in the decade 1932-42, but only ever mentions trips from Flatts to Hamilton as being by carriage or cycle. Like most Bermudians of that time, he courted his wife with countless miles of pedalling.

In practice, therefore, this was a single track without branch lines and, on the whole, it failed to attract regular patronage from those who did not live conveniently close by. These proved to be potential customers, lost.

16. A view along Front Street, Hamilton — undated photo by Knudson

17. 'The Square', Hamilton, from the sun deck of a cruise ship — c. June 1930

Bermuda Archives

18. The train on Front Street, Hamilton — undated photo c.1937

Bermuda Archives

19. A group of sailors prepares to tour Hamilton — undated, c.1942

20. Military band on train — photo from Major Moore Collection, 1943

21. Railway wagon on track — taken by visitor John Petersen, July 1944

22. The train passes through Southampton countryside — undated c.1944

23. Overlooking Great Sound from Black Bay Station — Rutherford photo

24. Bicycles parked on Queen Street, Hamilton — Vilzak photo 1938

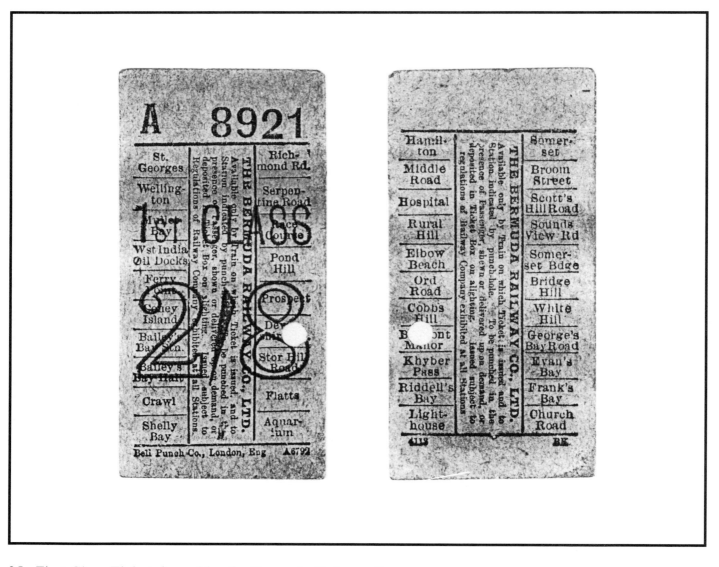

25. First Class Ticket, issued by the Bermuda Railway Company

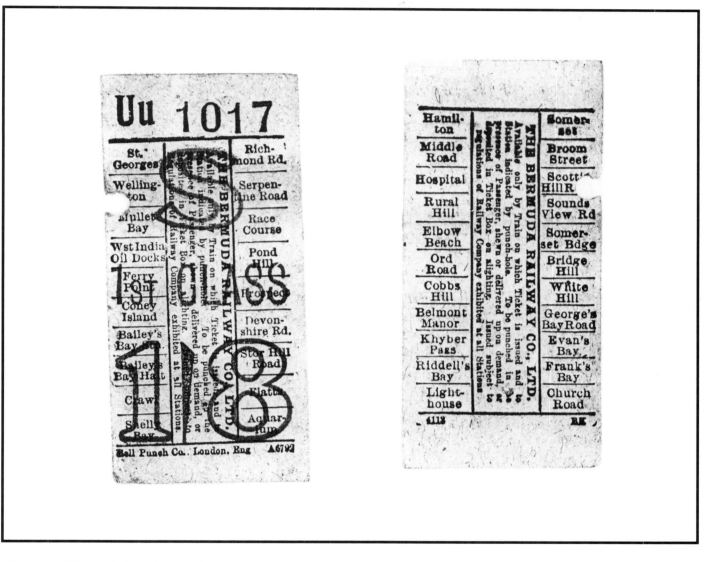

26. First Class Ticket, issued by the Bermuda Railway Company

City of Hamilton Waterfront, Bermuda.

27. Bermuda Railway postcard — circa 1933

28. Bermuda Railway postcard — circa 1938

One Final Chug to the Terminal

The demise of the Bermuda Railway had been expected ever since the end of the Second World War. On the one hand, it was becoming painfully obvious that the entire system was in desperate need of a major overhaul; on the other, profit margins had always been so minimal that it was failing clearly as a business venture. Without the availability of funds to finance the necessary repairs, a spiralling descent into hopelessness became unavoidable.

It had been no secret that the financial security of the 'Bermuda Railway Company' had been in doubt throughout most of its operational existence. Other than disappointing receipts from fares, there was a lengthening trail of small yet revealing cutbacks and cost-cutting measures.

Apart from regular day-to-day expenses for fuel, wages, advertising, servicing and rents, there was a miscellany of other payments to be met. Certainly many of these were small, but collectively they became a heavy burden to a company which was financially insecure. For example, the original 'Bermuda Railway Company Act 1924' (section 15, part 2) stipulated that the railway, as a public service, had to be monitored by a body of Railway Commissioners; the company was responsible for funding half of their annual operating budget. On 17th. January 1938, therefore, Colonial Treasurer John Trimingham invoiced the company for reimbursement of its share of the 1937 costs of 224.4.2d. Although this sum fell to 153 pounds in 1940, the company still was obligated to paying its share: rent for the Commissioners' office amounted to 12 pounds per annum; the secretary's wage came to 90 pounds and diverse fees accumulated to 42 pounds.

As yet a further indicator of its crippling financial plight, an internal memorandum dated 16th. February 1946, notes that the Ferry Point swing bridge operator, Mr. J. H. Outerbridge, had been called for Jury Duty; who, therefore, was responsible for his weekly wage of 4.18.0d.? Similarly worried about another expense, on 19th. July 1946 the company approached the Colonial Secretary expressing concern about the 300 pounds rent being paid annually for its ten-room offices on Reid Street. Rather boldly, the company pleaded that it could reduce these costs if space could be found in the 'Hamilton Princess Hotel', for 12 rooms! Furthermore, wages for skilled labour had increased recently to 25 shillings per day - as had occurred for St. George Corporation mechanic Mr. Ivan Smith. Who could afford to pay them?

Perhaps the first true nail in the proverbial coffin came in the form of a letter written by the Bermuda Government on 6th. February 1946, addressed to 'Sandon and Fitzpatrick', consulting engineers in New York. The two partners in this highly respected Park Avenue firm were James F. Sanborn and Edward B. Fitzpatrick. At the request of the Transport Control Board, they, were invited to undertake a thorough study of the rails, rolling stock, bridges and trestles of the railway and to compile a report on the overall condition of the entire facility. Under the terms of a signed agreement, the consultants were asked not only to assess the status of the system itself, but also to estimate the costs likely to be incurred by its repair and restoration. Perhaps more significantly, however, a second phase requested an estimate of the costs needed to prepare the railway bed itself for conversion into a highway — to be used by motor vehicles. This was the first full survey ever undertaken since the railway opened, but for the future of poor old "Shake and Rattle", this latter objective loomed ominously indeed.

With praiseworthy efficiency, inspection commenced on 26th. March 1946. Fieldwork was completed by 3rd. April 1946 and the finished report was presented to Government on 20th. May 1946. In their final report, the consulting engineers provided an itemized breakdown of the condition of each of the 33 individual bridges and trestles, and furnished a map (appended as Plate II) to show the precise location of each one. There were fully comprehensive explanations of every single major finding, and these revelations were coupled to statistical analyses contained in a 'Tables of Estimates'. The Government was well pleased with the paper cumbersomely identified as "Report on Railway Studies to the Bermuda Transport Control Board May 20th. 1946."

The document was concise and thorough. It indicated that not only had the 'Sanborn and Fitzpatrick' field staff been meticulous in their inspections, but that they had also conducted thoughtful and extensive interviews with company staff. In particular close contact had been maintained with Harold Rolling Kitchen, the long-serving Chief Engineer of the 'Bermuda Railway Company' — and perhaps its leading authority. Harold Kitchen had been one of the principal designers of the rolling stock and had served as Chief Engineer throughout its operation. His son William Kitchen, for several years, had worked alongside his father as a senior assistant. Their input was vital to any evaluations.

James Sanborn had collated incoming information from Bermuda. Simultaneous to these 'in situ' investigations, partner Edward Fitzpartick had sat at his desk in New York patiently examining every available item of pertinent published material, including a variety of research papers, diagrams and charts. Among the documents he read were: 'Revised Trestle Alignments', a paper published in February 1931 by 'Balfour Beatty and Co. Ltd.'; 'Profile of Location" (a series of drawings from April 1932); 'Final Report of the Commission on Public Transport' (dated .January 1945) compiled by Bermuda's Transport Control Board; and a recent publication entitled 'Expenditure on Maintenance of Permanent Way and Rolling Stock', written by an economist named Bergsrom in 1945.

'Sanborn and Fitzpatrick' also took the trouble to study a series of Ordnance Charts compiled in 1899. These showed the actual alignment of railway, stations, bridges and trestles, as plotted on a map surveyed originally by a Public Works Department employee affectionately named Mr. "Horsey" Stables. He had produced his charts for the first detailed railway feasibility study ever undertaken by the Bermudian Government — well before the eventual introduction of any railway — and Stables' surveys were, therefore, full of significant topographical data and observations.

The body of the final report was an amalgam of statistics and comments, the majority of which must have surely distressed railway company officials and investors. Because it was destined to be the last indepth study of the railway, it provided a most intimate picture of Bermuda's railway, immediately prior to its untimely demise.

Alas! The picture painted by the compilers was not one indicating the sort of mild sickness which could be easily fixed by prescribing a simple tonic; rather, it exposed the pressing need for radical surgery. From the outset, it methodically revealed that some degree of deterioration had been detected in 50% of the track hardware; 45% of the sills had deteriorated, as well as 85% of the track caps and 20% of all braces. The timbers in the trestles fared no better. Here, the inspectors determined that virtually three-quarters of all woodwork was in dire need of either repair or complete replacement.

Having made extensive use of wood in constructing every bridge, overpass and trestle, the original contractors were now faulted for the single-minded, short-sightedness of their designs. "Once deterioration has set in," the report warned, "the actual extent of deterioration is invariably greater than careful inspection indicates." Furthermore, it stated, "deterioration progresses at an accelerating rate!" With continuing criticism, the inspectors highlighted the fact that all trestle timbers had been trimmed to size and creosoted, prior to their actual shipment to Bermuda. This meant, therefore, that not only had deterioration actually begun before their very arrival at the local dockside, but that subsequent on site trimming had inevitably resulted in these fresh, completely untreated ends of timber being left exposed to the salty elements.

Striking a similarly disturbing chord, the report raised the possibility of yet another dubious and inferior building practice, by recommending that all correctly – mixed concrete should be made with freshwater — intimating that the original contractors may have made extensive and expedient use of saltwater during the pouring of some pillars and foundations. A cardinal sin if ever there was one!

Messrs. Sanborn and Fitzpatrick complained that the records of the 'Bermuda Railway Company' revealed no satisfactory details regarding the upkeep costs for the trestles during the preceding fifteen years. For this reason, therefore, they were unable to fully determine the real extent and effectiveness of any preservative measures that had been undertaken to retard timber deterioration. In closing this section on the general condition of all woodwork, the engineers forlornly remarked that: "repairs to the existing structures, no matter how promptly and carefully made, would have only temporary value." In essence, repairs would serve merely as a bandaid; their lifetime still could be expected to exceed no more than another two or three years. For this short-term remedy, the raw lumber alone would probably cost about $20,000.

The bottom line to this complete evaluation was no less discouraging. Required by the terms of reference to submit an estimate of costs, the report proposed that close to a quarter-of-a-million dollars would be needed to build new trestles and cut safer embankments. To replace the bridge at Flatts it was figured that $40,000 would be needed; a new bridge over to Coney Island was given a price tag $18,000. Repairs to the Evans Pond Trestle were calculated at $17,000; the one at "Riddells Bay", just $10,000. The cost of replacing the Springfield Trestle, at the Foot-of-the-Lane, was estimated at $30,000.

Reading through the report for the first time, the Railway Commissioners found hardly anything in its contents to comfort or console. Barely halfway through its pages, the inspectors had already predicted that "unless the repairs are made, traffic on the railway will have to be suspended until new structures have been completed."

More pragmatically, officials at the Transport Control Board eagerly turned to the Part II of the report, where they hoped to find support for the plan to turn the railway bed into a highway for motorized vehicles. This, it was now decided, was probably the mode of transport for the future. The railway had failed to prove itself, despite the genuine optimism with which it had been launched.

This second portion of the study began by defining the parameters within which the compilers had worked. Calculations concerning the new roadways had all been based on one set of guidelines: a maximum width of 18 feet; bituminous macadam surfaces correctly constructed for proper drainage; speeds not in excess of 30 miles per hour; bridges designed to carry 10 ton trucks; roads designed for 7 ton trucks; no pedestrian walkways, nor lighting to be provided.

Commencing with the removal of the existing train tracks, it was estimated that this could be achieved for about $100,000 — of which half might be recouped through the sale of scrap metal and salvaged timbers. Based on the previous determination that seventeen of the thirty-three bridges and trestles would need to be completely replaced, it was estimated that the construction of replacements, new landfills and new embankments would amount to $526,000. Alternatively, sixteen of the bridges could be demolished and replaced with custom-designed highway bridges, at a cost of $998,000; of this amount, perhaps approximately $70,000 could be realized from the sale of salvaged timber and steel. In the case of the bridge at Flatts, the report noted that this expense could be eliminated entirely, if the road was routed directly through Flatts Village instead.

Converting the existing railway route into a highway, an idea widely favoured in local transportation circles, was estimated at a probable cost of $1,819,000. The cost of restoring the entire railway system to a first class condition was estimated at $850,000.

In its closing paragraphs the report chose to quote the impartial opinion of James Sanborn and Edward Fitzpatrick. The respected engineering consultants suggested: "Because of the prohibitive cost and because the highway would not provide the public any better general transportation than the railway, we are bound to conclude that it would not be feasible to convert the existing railroad bed into a highway for the use of motor vehicles." In short, whilst any repairs to the present railway would be far from permanent, if the country was now moving towards adopting a policy based on replacing trains with automobiles, then it would be far wiser to develop a new system of roads — rather than trying to follow train tracks. What was seen initially as an expedient measure, was now cast as naively impractical; obviously, the needs of cars and trains were entirely different.

With the 'Report on Railway Studies' formally presented to Parliament and reviewed in the daily newspapers, street corner debaters concurred with the emerging feeling that perhaps the railway had been a mistake in the first place. Maybe the likes of Sir Stanley Spurling, as he now was, had been correct by proposing back in 1925, that carriage congestion could be relieved best by using motor cars. On hindsight, the entire railroad experiment had hardly proved to be the roaring financial success which its promoters had anticipated.

Pessimistically, the Colonial Secretary sent a letter to the Public Transport Board noting that the permit issued for the 'Bermuda Railway Company' to exhibit advertisements in its carriages was due to expire on 31st. December 1946. It was almost as if he didn't expect anybody to apply for a renewal.

By now, safety was rapidly emerging as another daily concern. Since 23rd. July 1945, the company had been aware that it would eventually have to close sections of track for the purposes of repair work. Indeed, on that date they had questioned the Government on whether they were legally allowed to drive passengers around out-of-service stretches of track, by lorry. In his reply, Colonial Secretary William Addis stated that there was "no authority under existing law to enable the 'Bermuda Railway Company' to carry passengers by truck in the event that any part of the railway line is temporarily closed to normal operation". That predicament alone was the source of considerable worry.

In 1946, faced with diminishing confidence in the railway's ability to function with safety, and in a gesture which denoted Government's desire to safeguard the country's main form of public transport, Parliament voted to purchase the track and rolling stock from the 'Bermuda Railway Company'. For the bargain basement price of just 150,000 pounds, the Bermuda Government found itself the proud owner of a desperately deteriorating railway system, one whose future was blatantly bleak. Obviously, it was a move of desperation, with little likelihood that the prevailing, distressing trends might be reversed. Following the release of the 'Sanborn-Fitzpatrick Report', the Government now faced the predicament of a repair and restoration bill officially estimated at close to one million dollars. It was quite obvious that the Government had inherited a dying horse; now, on an almost daily basis, hopes grew dimmer that any profit could ever realized on this brazen investment of public money.

Paralleling these continually emerging dilemmas was growing concern over the incidence of accidents and dangers, many of which could be directly attributed to the faulty condition of railway equipment. On 21st. April 1947, a voucher was issued to cover the medical treatment provided by Dr. R. E. Nash to conductor F. Lema, who had been "injured while on duty." The following month, on 20th. April 1947, mechanic W. W. Lovell applied for reimbursement for a prescription filled by the Phoenix Drug Store, following a minor work-related injury. These were only two of several, but signposted the likelihood that increases in accident expenses should be anticipated.

One indirect consequence of this steady rise in the issue of medical vouchers, was the drafting of several amendments to 'The Public Officers and Employees Injuries Relief Act'. As the employer of railway workers, Government was becoming remarkably security conscious.

In January 1947, the nominal shareholders and other company representatives gathered to assess the future. No one saw the mythical cloud with a silver lining. Indeed, the outlook was decidedly glum.

Convening a meeting under the chairmanship of Vice President Sir Stanley Spurling, the mood was justifiably despondent about the inevitability of the conclusions which they must surely draw. For some, it was particularly hard. Geoffrey Palgrave Barker had held a share in the company since 24th. May 1928 and had secured three others as recently as 1945. Seated nearby, W. F. Goodwin Gosling had owned his share since 21st. June 1926. Sir Stanley himself had been a shareholder since 10th. December 1932, one year longer than William John Curtis. Wilfred John Davis had owned his share since 20th. November 1944. More recent shareholders included William Williamson, with one year standing, and James Younger, who had acquired his share only a month earlier, on 9th. December 1946. All of the other 10,105 registered shares had been the property of 'Trustees Corporation Limited', the group behind the full financial backing of the railway since 15th. March 1928. In reality, of course, the Government of Bermuda had become the leading shareholder.

After considering a host of stop gap measures, the Commissioners reluctantly declared that the 'Bermuda Railway Company' was no longer able to provide a safe and reliable alternative to local transportation needs; furthermore, they admitted its inability to operate as a viable business. Thereby, they conceded obliquely that the motor car had won the day.

Consequently, 1947 witnessed the passage of three pieces of legislation which effectively ground the former 'Bermuda Railway Company' to a halt: 'The Bermuda Railway (Management and Operation) Act 1947'; 'The Bermuda Railway (Management and Operation) Act 1946, Amendment Act 1947'; and the 'Abandonment of the Bermuda Railway Act 1947'.

Alongside service cutbacks, staff redundancies became unavoidable; former railways properties were converted to different uses. On 3rd. June 1947, the Reverend Father McCarthy was given permission to use one of the old freight sheds at Tiger Bay, for church bazaars. By 2nd. December, Mrs. Honeyborne had already taken over one of the offices near St. George terminal as a dispatching centre for her fledgling taxi service; changes were being considered to amend 'Traffic Order #1 1947' in order to provide more parking space for autocars in the old town. In .January 1948, Reverend J. W. Stow was given use of another freight shed at Tiger Bay, for weekly meetings of the Church Lads Brigade. Three months later, Sir Stanley Spurling was granted approval to build an 'Esso' gas station on his property at Rose Hill, in St. George. With the budding popularity of automobiles, the demand for such a service became essential.

In what was to become one of the most ironic rings of change, it was none other that Mr. Harold Rolling Kitchen who was retained by 'Watlington & McPhee' to study the introduction of a bus service into St. George. It was Kitchen who duly proposed that buses should enter singly along York Street and off load passengers in King's Square; after parking for five minutes, outgoing passengers would embark in the square and buses would leave via the same route. The man whose name had been so long associated with the railway, had now applied his talents to a bus system. Instead of plotting the locations of train stations, it was now he who toyed with where to erect bus shelters and waiting rooms.

In 1947, Bermuda turned its head towards planning celebrations to mark the uncoming marriage between H. R. H. Princess Elizabeth and H. R. H. Prince Philip; legislators had already begun to fine-tune the 'Motor Car Act 1946 and, in the next parliamentary session, intended to introduce new measures to regulate cars. Already the Mayors of Hamilton and St. George had begun conferring on what road improvements might be needed, should it prove viable to land freight by aeroplane at the new civil air terminal. The railway appeared to have no place in the scheme of things to come.

In 1948, the Transport Board insured its fleet of 28 motorised vehicles. Sadly, for the first time in nearly seventeen years, no insurance coverage was requested or issued for any trains.

The Bermuda Government negotiated its sale to British Guiana. All over the island trestles and bridges were removed; track was prised from sleepers; metal plates and spikes were tossed into stacks among the undergrowth; piles of rotten timber were put up for bid.

The dismantling of the railway system was undertaken by 'Salisbury Construction' throughout 1948. In October of that year, that company's President, Mr. William Diel, met with Colonel R. V. Teart, General Manager of 'The British Guiana Transport and Harbour Department', to discuss details concerning its shipment from Bermuda to South America. The bulk of the track and rolling stock was subsequently carried aboard the vessel 'Pachita', which made several visits here in 1948. The cargo was assigned to 'The Demerara Railroad Company' in Georgetown, whose responsibility the dismembered railway had now become.

Quietly, an era had ended; and the Bermuda Railway ceased to exist.

On 14th. September 1952, the 'Royal Gazette' carried a feature article under the banner headline "Bermuda's old Railway is still going Strong". The item referred to the summer visit which the Headmaster of Whitney Institute had just made to British Guiana, during which he has seen the faithful train "connecting many small villages along the coast". He reported that the railway was playing a major role in developing a transport network in its adopted country — news which was welcomed by Bermudians, who had so frequently wondered about the well-being of their dear old 'Rattle and Shake'.

THE WAY IT IS TODAY

29. The Tiger Bay Station, St. George

30. Route of the railway track along Ferry Reach

31. An abandoned railway station at West India Oil Docks

32. Remains of the Ferry Reach Bridge

33. Concrete supports of Coney Island Bridge

34. Trestle foundations at Bailey's Bay

35. Aquarium Station, now the Bermuda Railway Museum

36. The bridge across Flatts Inlet

37. Along the northern entry into Hamilton, near Bull's Head

38. Railway cutting and underpass at Rural Hill, Paget

39. Road and railway cutting near Church Road, Southampton (see photo 6)

40. Concrete supports at Frank's Bay (see photo 4)

41. Railway station and platform along Georges Bay Road, Southampton

42. Scene near Somerset Bridge

43. Railway cutting near 'Lantana', Sandys

44. Railway route along the Great Sound, Somerset

45. The railway terminal in Somerset

APPENDIX 1

Acts associated with the Bermuda Railway, and related Topics

Sources: "The Statute Law of Bermuda (Private Acts 1709-1953 Vol. I)".
                "Private Acts 1930 - Volume III':
                "Public Acts, 1946":

#17 1924 - 'Bermuda Railway Company Act, 1924' (4th. August 1924) - p.463; petition presented in name of Robert Augustus Cummings; this Act accepted the formation of a company and granted approval for it "to acquire compulsorily the land required for the undertaking"; it gave the Company exclusive rights to operate a rapid transit rail system (Full text 1930 Vol. III p.449)

#9   1925 - 'Bermuda Railway Company Act, 1925'

#45 1925 - 'Bermuda Railway Company Act - #2, 1925'; (22nd. Dec. 1925) - p.482; these Acts required the Company to survey a route and present a plan to the Governor, on a scale not less than 6" per mile; the Company was also permitted to make drilling and sample testings as might relate to the suitability of the proposed route;

#52 1927 - 'Bermuda Railway Company Act, 1927'; (19th. Dec. 1927) - p.510; this Act extended the time originally specified for the start of construction;

#27 1929 - 'Bermuda Railway Company Act, 1929'; (22nd. June 1929) - p.526; this Act amended the procedure required for the Company to acquire land and also extended the construction period; one clause related to loan repayments;

#41 1930 - 'Bermuda Railway Company Act, 1930'; (12th. June 1930) - p.550; this was an Amendment permitting a change of route, in light of the Government's proposal to convert Pembroke East Marsh into a Recreation Ground;

#24 1931 - 'Bermuda Railway Company Act, 1931'; (20th. May 1931) - p.557; this was a Petition from Acting-Secretary of the B. R. Co. (Mr. Frederick MacFarlane) seeking to avoid any technical breaches of the '1923 Companies Act', as regards the composition and constitution of the B. R. Co.;

#46 1931 - 'Bermuda Railway Company Act, 1931'; (9th. Dec. 1931) - p.562; this refers to a Minute provided by the Department of Public Works, recommending an extension of the building period for the railway;

#2   1932 - 'Bermuda Railway Company Refund Act'; (29th. Jan. 1932) - p.563; this refers to a refund of 20,000 pounds sterling to the manager of Lloyds Bank in London, by the 'Bermuda Traction Company', on behalf of the B. R. Co., with interest, as agreed in the 1929 Act;

#45 1933 - 'Bermuda Railway Company Act, 1933'; (4th. Aug. 1933) - p.584; required the B. R. Co. to present its Accounts to the Railway Commissioners within 60 days of 30th. June each year;

#46 1935 - 'Bermuda Railway Company Act, 1935'; (9th. Dec. 1935) - p.614; this exempted the Company from all taxes for the year 1935;

#62   1941 -   'Bermuda Railway Company Act, 1941'; (23rd. Dec. 1941) - p.698; this exempted the Company from all taxes for the year 1941;

#58   1944 -   'Bermuda Railway Company Act, 1944'; (27th. Dec. 1944) - p.731; this exempted the Company from all taxes for the year 1944;

#23   1945 -   'The Bermuda Airways Limited Act, 1945' - p.731 - passed 26th. May 1945; John Ernest Peniston Vesey, Arthur John Graham, Edward Arthur Goodeve, Morris Alvin Gibbons, petitioned the Government to allow them to form a joint stock company — to have a capital of not less than 5,000 pounds and not more than 300,000 pounds: "to acquire, purchase, operate, sell, lease out and repair aircraft of any description, to operate such aircraft for the conveyance of passengers, freight and mails within these islands, or to and from places outside these islands." (Full text in Vol. I page 748).

#39   1945 -   'The Bermuda Omnibus Company Act, 1945' - p.746; passed 17th. August 1945; The Bermuda Railway Company Ltd. and the Bermuda Transportation Company Ltd. petitioned to form a joint stock company for the purposes of operating an Omnibus Company.

#3   1946 -   'The Railway Purchase Act, 1946' - repealed 1951 - Public Act;

#4   1946 -   'The Operation of the Bermuda Railway Act, 1946' - repealed 1946 - Public Act;

#8   1946 -   'The Motor Transport Company Act, 1946' - Private Act - 18th. Feb. 1946; "Whereas the B. R. Co. Ltd. and the Bermuda Transportation Company Ltd. have presented a Petition to the Legislature setting forth that they have agreed to form a joint stock company to be called the 'Motor Transportation Co. Ltd.' for the purpose herein expressed and that the petitioners are desirous of having the said Company incorporated by an Act of the Legislature limiting the liability of the shareholders to the amount unpaid on their respective shares and praying that an Act may be passed to enable the said Company to become incorporated and to confer on the said Company certain powers necessary for the carrying on of its business, and it is deemed expedient to pass an Act for such purposes." (For full text see 1946 Volume, page 25)

#46   1946 -   'The Public Transportation Board Act, 1946' - repealed 1951 - Public Act;

#14   1946 -   'The Operation of the Bermuda Railway Act, 1946' - Public Act;

#46   1946 -   'The Motor Car Act, 1946' - repealed 1951 - Public Act;

#77   1947 -   'The Bermuda Railway (Management and Operation) Act, 1947' - Public Act - expired;

#38   1947 -   'The Bermuda Railway (Management and Operation) Act, 1946. Amendment Act, 1947' - repealed 1951 - Public Act;

#46   1947 -   'The Abandonment of the Bermuda Railway Act, 1947' - Public Act - repealed 1951

#29   1949 -   'The Bermuda Motor and Cycle Accessories Co. Ltd. Act, 1949' - p.929; passed

12th. May 1949; Reid Conway Mayor Trott and Laurion Ewing Trott petitioned Parliament to have the Company incorporated by an Act of Legislature; the Company to have, among other things, exclusive rights to the name of the Company and to allow it to: acquire and erect filling stations, repair shops, to purchase and acquire and sell and repair parts and accessories for mechanically propelled vehicles of all descriptions, cycles, boats, ships and aircraft. (page 929 Volume II)

#55 1951 - 'Radio Programmes and Facilities Act, 1951' - p.1184; passed 22nd. June 1951; William Charles Cran and Sir Edwin Savory Herbert petitioned the Legislature to allow them to form a joint stock company to operate, sell advertising time, acquire and create recorded programmes.

#6 1953 - 'The Bermuda Air Tours and Flying School Act, 1953' - p.1321; passed 28th. Jan. 1953; Herbert Fortesque Watlington and Janet Lilian Watlington petitioned the Legislature to allow them to form a Company with a capital of not less than 3,000 pounds - to take over and operate all services, real estate of "Bermuda Air Tours" owned by H. F. Watlington and to expand the provisions to include instruction and flying schools and instruction in repairs.

#26 1953 - 'The Auto, Bicycles and Auxiliary Bicycles Special Measures of Control Act, 1953' - p.103 of 1953 Book;

1953 - 'The Motor Car Act 1951, Amendment Act 1953';